When one thinks of horses, words such as strength and majesty are often cons
assisted interventions have developed over the past fifty years and are becoming
as a form of therapy. Hallberg's book and companion workbook are excellent sour
how trained horses and professionals can work together to support the quality o
The book and the accompanying workbook are a must for all interested professio.
Aubrey H. Fine, EdD, *licensed psychologist/professor at Cal Poly State University, editor/author of* The Handbook on Animal Assisted Therapy, How Animals Help Students Learn, *and* Afternoons with Puppy

Leif Hallberg's *The Equine-Assisted Therapy Workbook* is the perfect companion to *The Clinical Practice of Equine-Assisted Therapy* as it provides readers with an informative and thought-provoking resource that addresses the scope, provision, business, ethics, and science of incorporating horses within health care.
Wendy Wood, PhD, OTR/L, FAOTA, *professor of Occupational Therapy, director of Research at the Temple Grandin Equine Center, Colorado State University*

This companion to *The Clinical Practice of Equine-Assisted Therapy* is easy to use and full of opportunities for self-paced, continued learning.
Nina Ekholm Fry, MSSc, CCTP, *director of Equine Programs & Equine-Assisted Mental Health, Institute for Human-Animal Connection, University of Denver*

The Equine-Assisted Therapy Workbook encourages readers to grow to be professionals in the EAT field, and to think and rethink their methodology, ethics, terminology, education, and practice. The workbook is written objectively stating Leif Hallberg's true understanding of EAT with all the twists. Hand in hand with the workbook goes *The Clinical Practice of Equine-Assisted Therapy* that targets the defining differences between the "branches" of EAA/EAT. Both the book and the workbook can be utilized internationally in teaching and self-learning.
Sanna Mattila-Rautiainen, *president of the Horses in Education and Therapy International Federation (HETI)*

Using *The Equine-Assisted Therapy Workbook* together with *The Clinical Practice of Equine-Assisted* Therapy will provoke industry wide self-reflection, and help both therapy and non-therapy professionals identify and advocate for their important and unique roles within this field.
Kitty Stalsburg, *PATH Intl. master instructor, ESMHL, CBEIP-ED, and executive director of High Hopes Therapeutic Riding, Inc.*

The Equine-Assisted Therapy Workbook

The Equine-Assisted Therapy Workbook gives readers the tools they need to increase professional competency and personalize the practical applications of equine-assisted therapy. Each chapter includes thought-provoking ethical questions, hands-on learning activities, self-assessments, practical scenarios, and journal assignments applicable to a diverse group of healthcare professionals. The perfect companion to *The Clinical Practice of Equine-Assisted Therapy*, this workbook is appropriate for both students and professionals.

Leif Hallberg, MA, LPC, LCPC, is an internationally acclaimed author, consultant, licensed mental health professional, and educator whose career has centered on the practice of equine-assisted activities and therapies. She is the author of *Walking the Way of the Horse: Exploring the Power of the Horse-Human Relationship*. Leif provides consultation services, offers individual sessions, teaches courses, and leads professional development trainings and workshops both nationally and internationally. She can be reached at www.leifhallberg.com.

The Equine-Assisted Therapy Workbook

A Learning Guide for Professionals and Students

Leif Hallberg

NEW YORK AND LONDON

First published 2018
by Routledge
711 Third Avenue, New York, NY 10017

and by Routledge
2 Park Square, Milton Park, Abingdon, Oxon, OX14 4RN

Routledge is an imprint of the Taylor & Francis Group, an informa business

Library of Congress Cataloging-in-Publication Data
A catalog record for this book has been requested

ISBN: 978-1-138-21612-9 (hbk)
ISBN: 978-1-138-21619-8 (pbk)
ISBN: 978-1-315-40226-0 (ebk)

Typeset in Garamond
by Apex CoVantage, LLC

Cover image: © "Majesty" by Laurie Pace, www.lauriepace.com

Contents

Foreword

Ms. Hallberg's *Equine-Assisted Therapy Workbook: A Learning Guide for Professionals and Students* is an excellent resource for the next generation of professionals who will undoubtedly shape the future of this emerging and promising industry.

As I read this workbook, I was reminded of my own professional journey from a PATH Intl. certified adaptive riding instructor to a licensed professional counselor providing animal-assisted interventions in counseling with a variety of animal species. I wish an educational resource such as this had been available to me during my initial training, as I would have started my career with a much deeper understanding and appreciation for the wide variety of professional roles among providers of equine-assisted therapy.

I strongly believe that in order to best serve our clients, we must understand the roles and scope of practice of each type of equine-assisted therapy professional (counselor, psychologist, physical therapist, occupational therapist, speech therapist, etc.). This understanding allows us to deliver high quality services from the lens of our own professional identity and create meaningful and intentional collaborations with other professionals.

One of the particular strengths of this workbook is the degree to which universal core competencies are addressed and thoroughly discussed, therefore making this a valuable resource for many healthcare and human service professionals. These core competencies form the foundation for the effective and ethical provision of any type of animal-assisted intervention and include an in-depth species-specific knowledge of our animal partners, positive and relationship-based training techniques, and the ability to effectively incorporate animals and the farm milieu in a patient's treatment plan. Being competent in these areas allows professionals to provide safe and effective interventions while simultaneously advocating for the welfare of the therapy animal(s) involved.

While the specific details involved in how a professional translates the human-animal interaction into clinically-relevant treatment goals may vary widely based on patient needs, professional identity, and choice of therapy animal species, the core competencies required of all providers of animal-assisted interventions remain the same.

I sincerely hope that readers of this workbook will recognize the importance of appreciating the knowledge, skills, and attitudes that unite all animal-assisted therapy providers while attending to the development of their own discipline-specific skills. Such appreciation and development is absolutely crucial to the provider's ability to deliver ethical and effective services that ultimately elevate the professionalism of the field of animal-assisted interventions as a whole.

Thank you, Leif, for creating and providing such a valuable training resource for helping professionals of many disciplines. I look forward to using your text and workbook in my own Animal Assisted Therapy in Counseling classes to help my students develop their core competencies and further solidify their professional identities as providers of equine-assisted counseling services.

Leslie A. Stewart, PhD, LPC
Assistant Professor of Counseling, Idaho State University
Primary Author of the American Counseling Association's Competencies
for Providers of Animal Assisted Therapy in Counseling

Acknowledgements

Special thanks to Ian McNairy, without whom there would be no workbook; to John and Nancy Hallberg for their dedication and tireless support; and to Dr. Daniel Stroud, Dr. Leslie Steward, Clare Thomas-Pino, Jacqueline Tiley, Ann Kern-Godal, Kali Welch, and so many other professionals whose expertise and advice I have relied upon over the years and throughout this process. Thank you to artist Laurie Pace for granting me permission to use her beautiful art as the cover for the book. Finally, thank you to Anna Moore and the team at Routledge for making this project possible.

About the Author

Leif Hallberg, MA, LPC, LCPC, is an internationally acclaimed author, consultant, licensed mental health professional, educator, and avid lover of nature and animals. Her professional career and life's work have centered around researching the human-equine bond, and studying the practice of equine-assisted activities and therapies (EAAT). As a leading expert, innovator, and pioneer, she has developed a reputation over the past 20 years for her broad-reaching and objective study of the industry and dissemination of information. It has been Leif's goal to clarify, define, and objectively describe the complexity and diversity of the human-equine relationship and the professional applications of this relationship.

A horseback riding instructor and horse trainer turned licensed mental health professional and educator, Leif relies both upon practical equine knowledge and her clinical experience to design innovative programs for a wide range of populations. Leif designs curricula and teaches courses and workshops at both an undergraduate and graduate level, and provides continuing education opportunities for professionals, presenting both nationally and internationally. Leif's books, *Walking the Way of the Horse: Exploring the Power of the Horse-Human Relationship* and *The Clinical Practice of Equine-Assisted Therapy: Including Horses in Human Healthcare* are used by colleges, universities, and training programs around the world.

Today, Leif provides consultation services, offers individual sessions, teaches courses, and leads professional development trainings and workshops both nationally and internationally. She can be reached at www.leifhallberg.com.

Introduction

Equine-assisted therapy is provided in over 50 countries around the world. This term broadly refers to any type of therapy or treatment that includes equine interactions, activities, treatment strategies, and the equine milieu. Services are regulated by healthcare laws and provided by appropriately educated, trained, and credentialed (licensed or registered) healthcare professionals. Typically, physical therapists, occupational therapists, speech therapists, mental health professionals, nurses, and—on some occasions—medical doctors are the licensed healthcare professionals who most commonly provide some form of equine-assisted therapy.

In order to ethically and safely provide equine-assisted therapy, professionals should seek additional training, education, supervision, and—in some cases—certification to advance their competency. This workbook is designed to accompany *The Clinical Practice of Equine-Assisted Therapy: Including Horses in Human Healthcare*, and its aim is to increase professional competency and enhance the reader's overall understanding of equine-assisted therapy while offering opportunities for continued learning, personal exploration, and professional development. It exposes readers to thought-provoking ethical questions, hands-on learning activities, self-assessments, practical scenarios, and journal assignments.

Using the book and the workbook together emphasizes the importance of being an active learner, and engaging in critical thinking and self-assessment. The workbook can accompany academic courses, professional development workshops, industry certificate programs, or can be used by anyone interested in furthering their own education and learning.

This workbook is applicable for physical therapists, occupational therapists, speech therapists, mental health professionals, nurses, and other healthcare professionals interested in equine-assisted therapy. It can be beneficial for both those new to the industry and professionals already providing services.

The workbook's outline directly mirrors the chapters in *The Clinical Practice of Equine-Assisted Therapy: Including Horses in Human Healthcare*, and each workbook chapter includes the following sections:

- Chapter Summary—Includes a brief overview of the content presented in *The Clinical Practice of Equine-Assisted Therapy: Including Horses in Human Healthcare*.
- Key Concepts—Highlights important points extracted from each chapter of the book.
- Learning Objectives—Guides the reader toward expected learning outcomes.
- Relevant Terminology—Introduces terms used in the workbook chapter that the reader may not be familiar with. In some cases, terms are repeated in multiple chapters to help remind the reader of the term's meaning.

- Questions to Explore—Offers thought-providing questions designed to help readers think critically about the book's content. Readers may also find they need to reference other materials included in the "Resource" section of the chapter to adequately answer these questions.
- Practical Scenarios—Affords opportunities to practically apply content in a variety of ways.
- Self-Assessments—Encourages thoughtful and honest assessment of knowledge and skills. Not every chapter includes a self-assessment.
- Hands-On Activities—Includes both equine activities to enhance the reader's relationship with horses, and community-based learning opportunities where readers investigate the professional practice of equine-assisted therapy.
- Journal Entries—Prompts the exploration of thoughts, feelings, and personal reflections.
- Resources—Provides additional resources to expand the learning process.

Internationalism and Equine-Assisted Therapy

It is the intention of this author to be inclusive of the many ways people practice in different countries around the world. However, due to the variations in law and practical application between countries, the level of specification needed to accurately craft scenarios or use language that would be inclusive of all countries was impossible to achieve in this workbook.

With that being said, it is hoped that readers will broadly apply the material within the context of their own laws, ethics, and standards of practice, and that they are welcome to adapt terms or scenarios as needed to be better representative of their cultures and countries.

Future Editions

With each new addition of *The Clinical Practice of Equine-Assisted Therapy: Including Horses in Human Healthcare*, this workbook will be reviewed for relevance and any necessary changes will be implemented. Future workbooks may also be developed that focus on specific areas of practice within equine-assisted therapy.

☐ How to Use the Workbook

In order to respond to the questions, practical scenarios, and the final exam, the reader must have read or be able to reference *The Clinical Practice of Equine-Assisted Therapy: Including Horses in Human Healthcare*. Additional resources are provided at the end of each workbook chapter, and in some cases, information that will help the reader to answer questions more thoroughly can only be found in these resource materials, and is not included in depth in either the book or the workbook. This is done to help expand the learning opportunities.

The workbook is designed as an active, hands-on learning tool. Readers can photocopy self-assessments, assignments, and the equine evaluation, or they can write directly in the workbook, answering questions or taking notes in the spaces allowed for this purpose. Readers are urged to take the workbook with them during site visits and professional interviews. They may also need to purchase a journal or use another notebook to accompany the workbook as the professional interview questions, journal entries, and other personal reflections generally require more space than is provided.

Activities

Each chapter in the workbook offers a hands-on learning activity. Some of these activities can be tailored to use clinically with patients. The intention is to expose the reader to these activities firsthand before they use the activity with patients. This allows the professional to consider what types of patients the activity might be suited for, how to adapt the activity for different patients, how the horses respond to the activity, how long the activity might take, and how difficult the activity is. It also gives professionals an opportunity to think about what treatment goals the activity could address, and how it might be best used in a treatment plan.

All of the activities that could be used clinically are highly adaptable to meet very different needs and abilities. For example, one activity deals with learning how to meet, greet, and move around a horse. This activity can be equally valuable in a physical therapy session for a child in a wheelchair with a moderate degree of cognitive function as it is in a mental health session for a high functioning woman dealing with depression. Professionals are urged to use this as an opportunity to think creatively, and envision how these and other activities could be used to address treatment goals.

Study Groups

It is recommended that readers who are not a part of an academic class or professional development workshop consider forming a study group to work through the material and activities included in this workbook. The learning opportunities will only be enhanced by discussion, peer interactions, and peer input.

☐ Biases and Beliefs Self-Assessment

This self-assessment is designed to encourage thoughtful and honest investigation into your own beliefs and biases as they relate to equine-assisted therapy. It will be provided at three different times during this workbook to help you gauge changes in your perception as you move through the workbook content. It is meant for your eyes only, although you may choose to use some of your responses in supervision, or discuss with peers as you feel comfortable. Try not to be judgmental of your responses, rather view this an opportunity to discover something new about yourself.

Rank the following statements accordingly: 1 = Strongly disagree, 2 = Disagree, 3 = Unsure or somewhere in the middle, 4 = Agree, 5 = Strongly agree. Total your score at the bottom of the self-assessment. A higher score indicates greater levels of acceptance, open-mindedness, and collaboration.

_____ I am open-minded and curious about how other people practice equine-assisted therapy.

_____ I research my beliefs, taking into consideration many different perspectives, and am comfortable changing my opinions based upon what I learn.

_____ I continually strive to learn more about equine-assisted therapy.

_____ I learn from other people's perspectives, and implement their ideas if applicable.

_____ I ask lots of questions and attempt to understand why other people think or believe the way they do.

_____ I see value in everyone's perspectives, and encourage open discussion about differences.

_____ I find collaboration refreshing, helpful, productive, and enjoyable.

_____ I enjoy and seek out collaborative environments or opportunities.

_____ I seek outside/expert support and guidance when making hard clinical decisions.

_____ I believe there are many different ways to work with horses, and I am open to trying new ideas.

_____ I seek outside/expert support and guidance when evaluating my horses' health and wellbeing.

_____ I take the advice of other people when it comes to addressing health and wellness issues with my horses.

_____ I make time to provide help and guidance to those new to the industry, and answer their questions with respect, patience, and open-mindedness.

_____ I welcome newcomers to the industry, and believe they have something to teach me.

_____ I am comfortable referring my patients to other professionals.

_____ When people ask me questions about equine-assisted therapy, I learn from their questions and find myself expanding my own knowledge because of their query.

_____ I make time to learn something new about equine-assisted therapy on a regular basis.

_____ I am easy to approach, and encourage conversation.

_____ I am less likely to judge people, and more likely to learn about them and their beliefs.

_____ I enjoy differences in beliefs, and find those differences valuable.

_____ I commonly use peer or professional supervision as a way to check my own decisions and beliefs.

_____ I use scholarly resources such as textbooks or peer-reviewed journals to inform my opinions and guide my decision making.

_____ I ask the opinions of others and listen to their advice, implementing applicable information.

_____ I am not defensive about my clinical decisions and am open to critique and suggestions.

_____ I am not defensive about my horse care decisions and am open to critique and suggestions.

_____ I don't assume equine-assisted therapy is right for every patient.

_____ I keep my personal beliefs about how horses might impact people out of the therapy process.

_____ I don't use equine-assisted therapy for every patient, and rather make careful choices about which patients would be best served by the treatment.

_____ I understand and value the investigative nature of equine-assisted therapy.

_____ I don't try to defend equine-assisted therapy as a "proven" clinical intervention, and if research results show less than positive effects, I am open and curious.

_____ I am able to separate my own love for horses from the clinical use of equine-assisted therapy.

_____ I provide equine-assisted therapy first because of the clinical benefits it offers the patient, and second because I enjoy it.

_____ I am open to the idea that working with another animal could produce health benefits similar to those of working with horses.

_____ I don't need my "way" of working with horses or providing equine-assisted therapy to be "right." I am open to many different approaches.

_____ I model collaborative values, believing this is important to teach patients as well as foster in other professionals.

_____ **TOTAL SCORE**

☐ Hands-On Activity: The Body Scan

Description: A very important first step in working with horses and people is being aware of yourself and learning how to regulate your own emotions. An increasing body of research suggests that both people and animals perceive subtle non-verbal communications or shifts in mood or emotion, and this can alter their responses and reactions. For example, if you are asking a horse to do something, and you notice the horse is being "difficult" and you stop to check in with yourself, you may realize you are actually feeling frustrated, irritable, or anxious about something that happened earlier that has nothing to do with the horse. Any of these emotions or feelings can impact how your horse reacts and responds to you, and thus change the outcome of the interaction.

The body scan is a mindfulness-based activity that promotes a greater sense of attunement with one's physical body while calming the mind and decreasing stress. It is not uncommon for therapists to experience a patient's physical or psychological stress or discomfort as manifested in their own bodies or states of emotion. The body scan helps therapists to identify how they are feeling, and can reduce emotional reactivity and combat the effects of stress or tension.

The first time doing the body scan it can be helpful to have someone walk you through the exercise using the following directions. Over time, you can establish your own unique way of doing a body scan that feels the most natural and helpful for you. This is only one example of hundreds of options for doing a body scan.

Amount of Time: 10 minutes every day, or multiple times a day as needed or desired.

Directions: Pick a quiet area where you will not be disturbed and stand with your feet hip-width apart and your hands hanging loosely by your sides. Close your eyes if you feel comfortable, otherwise allow your eyes to become soft. Take three deep breaths in your nose and release your breath out of your mouth.

1. Bring your attention to the soles of your feet. Wiggle your toes. See if you can feel all parts of your feet touching the earth.
2. Continue rhythmical deep breathing and gently move your focus up to your ankles, your shins, your calves, to your knees. Notice if you feel any pain or tension anywhere.
3. Continue up your body—thighs, buttocks, hips, abdomen, lower back, ribs, chest, mid-back, and shoulders. Breathe, roll your shoulders, and relax down. How do you feel? Where are you holding tension?
4. Continue down your arms, noticing your elbows, wrists, hands, and fingers. Breathe deeply, wiggle your figures, circle your wrists, and then move back up your arms to your neck, chin, jaw, cheeks, nose, eyes, eyebrows, forehead, and temple. Breathe deeply, rotate your neck, move your jaw side to side, and open and close your mouth. Feel your eyes, your face—are you holding tension there?
5. Finally, bring your attention to your head. Take three big deep breaths. Imagine a trap door opening up at the very top of your head. On an exhale, allow any tension to exit out through the trap door, releasing into the universe. Know the universe will take care of it in a good way.
6. When you are done, gently allow the trap door to close, bringing in with it radiant white light. Send this light down through your body, focusing on any of the places that held tension or pain. Bring the light all the way down to the soles of your feet, and picture it spreading

out from your feet into the earth below. Feel your body pulled tall with your head reaching towards the sky and your feet sinking into the earth. Take a few breaths in this position and relax your body.

7. Then, gently allow your senses to become attuned to the natural world. What do you hear? Smell? Taste? Feel? Allow yourself to become immersed in your environment. Breathe deeply, listen to the sounds of nature, experience the touch of the air.

8. When you are ready, allow your eyes to open and look around yourself with a soft eye. Take in all the colors, shapes, forms, sounds, and smells that make up your environment. Notice how you feel.

9. What message does your body have for you? How do you feel after the body scan? Where are you holding tension? Were you able to let go of some of the tension? If not, how is that tension serving you? Practice non-judgmental observation of your thoughts and feelings. There is nothing wrong with needing to hold onto things sometimes. Just notice.

☐ Journal Entry

Use these questions as an opportunity to explore your own ideas, thoughts, feelings, and personal reflections.

1. What did you notice when you did the body scan? How often do you slow down and check in with yourself? How might you use the body scan practice in daily life? How might you use this hands-on activity with patients?

_____

_____

_____

_____

2. Describe any personal beliefs and biases that may have arisen out of the self-assessment survey. How might these beliefs or biases impact your professional practice, your patients, or yourself?

_____

_____

_____

_____

3. How might your personal relationships with horses create biases about equine-assisted therapy, or impact your clinical work?

_____

_____

_____

_____

4. Why do you think it might be important to consider personal biases or beliefs as you begin this workbook?

_____

_____

_____

_____

☐ **Resources**

Books & Articles

American Psychological Association (APA). (2012). *What are the benefits of mindfulness?* Continuing Education Article. Retrieved from: www.apa.org/monitor/2012/07-08/ce-corner.aspx

Botha, E., Gwin, T., & Purpora, C. (2015). The effectiveness of mindfulness-based programs in reducing stress experienced by nurses in adult hospital settings: A systematic review of quantitative evidence protocol. *JBI Database of Systematic Reviews & Implementation Reports, 13*(10), 21–29. Retrieved from: http://journals.lww.com/jbisrir/Fulltext/2015/13100/The_effectiveness_of_mindfulness_based_programs_in.4.aspx

Coholic, D. (2010). *Arts activities for children and young people in need: Helping children to develop mindfulness, spiritual awareness and self-esteem.* London: Jessica Kingsley Publishers.

Gouda, S., Luong, M.T., Schmidt, S., & Bauer, J. (2016). Students and teachers benefit from mindfulness-based stress reduction in a school-embedded pilot study. *Frontiers in Psychology, 7,* 1–18. Retrieved from: www.ncbi.nlm.nih.gov/pmc/articles/PMC4845593/

Kabat-Zinn, J. (2012). *Mindfulness for beginners: Reclaiming the present moment—and your life.* Louisville, CO: Sounds True Inc.

Kabat-Zinn, J. (2013). *Full catastrophe living: Using the wisdom of your body and mind to face stress, pain, and illness* (Revised updated edition). New York: Bantam.

Kenga, S.-L., Smoskib, M.J., & Robins, C.J. (2013). Effects of mindfulness on psychological health: A review of empirical studies. *Clinical Psychological Review, 31*(6), 1041–1056. Retrieved from: www.ncbi.nlm.nih.gov/pmc/articles/PMC3679190/pdf/nihms463108.pdf

Markova, D., & McArthur, A. (2015). *Collaborative intelligence: Thinking with people who think differently.* New York: Spiegel & Grau.

Websites

UC Berkeley's Greater Good Science Center—the Hope Lab, Greater Good in Action https://ggia.berkeley.edu/
UCLA Mindfulness Research Center http://marc.ucla.edu/about-marc

1 Foundations of Equine-Assisted Therapy

☐ Chapter One Summary

For centuries, relationships with horses have been associated with human wellbeing. More recently, horses are included in physical, occupational, speech, and mental health therapy provided by licensed healthcare professionals.

Although people are drawn to the mystique, power, and beauty of horses and attribute healing qualities to the horse-human relationship, there is paucity of empirical research investigating the exact role of the horse as an agent of change. The few studies that have been conducted focus mostly on the movement of the horse, and how that movement affects the human body. Other than this research, anecdotal reports suggest ethological characteristics of the horse may have a therapeutic effect on humans, including motivating them to engage more fully in treatment and encouraging a greater level of authenticity between patients and therapists.

As research demonstrates, it is difficult, if not impossible, to separate out the role of nature, the impact of the human-animal bond, and the many other co-occurring factors that exist in the dynamic and unpredictable farm environment or "milieu." Therefore, it is unknown if the horse is the sole agent of change during an equine-assisted therapy session. In fact, researchers recommend that future studies are designed to include control groups in which participants engage in nature-based activities at the farm without horses, or work with a different domesticated large prey animal, like a llama, goat, or cow. By doing this type of research, the role of the horse as a change agent can be further explored.

Assuming the benefits of equine-assisted therapy are enhanced by time spent outdoors in nature, and interactions with other animals, providers of equine-assisted therapy are encouraged to learn techniques that capitalize upon these therapeutic opportunities.

☐ Key Concepts

- Equine-assisted therapy is one type of animal-assisted therapy, and foundational theories related to human-animal bonding apply.
- Equine-assisted therapy also shares foundational theories with nature-based therapy, including the human need for connection to nature (biophilia), stress reduction theory, and attention restoration theory.
- Although research has established that relationships with companion animals like dogs and cats can be attributed to a variety of health benefits like lowered blood pressure and decreased risk of cardiovascular disease, these studies have not included horses, and thus the findings are not transferable. Additional research needs to be conducted to determine if relationships with horses have similar (or different) health benefits.

- The American Pet Partners model of animal-assisted therapy is different than the European model of care farming, in which animals are considered an important part of the farm environment, but are not "therapy animals." It is useful for providers of equine-assisted therapy to be familiar with both models.
- Including other species of animal or nature-based activities in equine-assisted therapy sessions can be therapeutically beneficial.
- Mounted work is the most well researched of all theories related to how horses might influence positive clinical change in humans, and research suggests that the movement of the horse can be an important treatment tool if appropriately used by a trained physical, occupational, or speech therapist.
- Mounted work should only be implemented after careful clinical assessment, as there are important considerations to take into account.
- While ethological characteristics of the horse like its sensitivity, communication style, and herd behaviors are widely discussed anecdotally in literature, these attributes are yet to be empirically studied as agents of clinical change.
- The excitement and novelty of working with or riding horses can help motivate patients to engage more fully in treatment, and can encourage more authentic relationships between patients and therapists.

☐ Learning Objectives

1. Identify different theories related to why horses may be included in human healthcare and examine ethical considerations.
2. Identify health benefits associated with human-animal interactions, describe the different forms of animal-assisted therapy, and discuss how theories of human-animal bonding may be implemented during equine-assisted therapy.
3. Identify key theories related to the role of nature in human health, and discuss ways to implement these theories during equine-assisted therapy.

☐ Relevant Terminology

Anecdotal Evidence: Is based upon personal experiences and testimonies, and is likely subjective in nature. Although scientists may use case studies and other formal ways of documenting people's experiences and testimonies in the process of conducting empirical research, lay people commonly use anecdotes to support their own beliefs that are not based in scientific method or study. The limitation of anecdotes as evidence is that they are not controlled and the outcomes could be affected by many hidden variables. Because of this, anecdotes are generally not considered definitive, and instead help guide the way for further empirical study.

Empirical Evidence: Is gained through observation and experimentation using specific research methods that ensure the accuracy, quality, and integrity of the data. Data is recorded and analyzed by scientists using the scientific method. Qualitative and quantitative methods are used to gather such empirical data.

Ethology: The scientific and objective study of animal behavior, especially under natural conditions.

Hippotherapy: Refers to how occupational, physical, and speech therapists incorporate equine movement and the farm milieu in a patient's treatment plan, using clinical reasoning in the purposeful manipulation of equine movement to engage sensory, neuromotor, and cognitive systems to achieve functional outcomes.

Nature-Based Therapies: Clinical interventions that utilize interactions with plants, animals and natural landscapes.

Surcingle: A strap that encircles the horse's girth right behind the withers. The surcingle can secure a pad to the horse's back, and can have handles (e.g. vaulting surcingle) that may provide additional support.

Withers: Usually the tallest point of the horse's back, immediately before the neck begins. A rider sits immediately behind the withers.

☐ Questions to Explore

Use information presented in *The Clinical Practice of Equine-Assisted Therapy: Including Horses in Human Healthcare*, the recommended resources provided in this chapter of the workbook, and your own knowledge and experience to reflect on the following questions.

1. Describe the foundational theories related to human-animal bonding and the human connection to nature. How do these theories relate to equine-assisted therapy?

   _____

   _____

   _____

   _____

2. Of the various ideas about how or why horses might be helpful or healing to humans, which do you (or might you) use most frequently in clinical work? Why? How does this change with different populations?

   _____

   _____

   _____

   _____

3. How can the movement of the horse impact the human body? How might you use this in your clinical practice? What ethical considerations should be taken into account?

   _____

   _____

   _____

   _____

4. Which ethological characteristics of horses do you find most impactful (for yourself or for patients)? What are the ethical considerations to take into account when considering the use of these equine characteristics for human health?

   _____

   _____

   _____

   _____

5. Considering the existing research, what health benefits are attributed to non-equine human-animal relationships? Pay special attention to which species of animal was studied, and discuss why researchers may have chosen the animals they did.

_____

_____

_____

_____

6. Describe the American Pet Partners model of animal-assisted therapy. Compare and contrast this model with the European care farming model and any other models of providing animal-assisted therapy you are familiar with. How do these models overlap with equine-assisted therapy?

_____

_____

_____

_____

7. How might you use animal-assisted therapy or even aspects of care farming in your equine-assisted therapy practice? What ethical considerations should be taken into account?

_____

_____

_____

_____

8. Considering the existing research, what health benefits are attributed to the human-nature relationship? What nature-based activities could you include in your equine-assisted therapy practice?

_____

_____

_____

_____

9. How might you capitalize upon the health-related benefits of human-animal-nature interactions? What ethical considerations should be taken into account?

_____

_____

_____

_____

☐ Practical Scenarios

Read the Scenarios and Answer the Following Questions.

Susan is a 24-year-old returning veteran. She was referred to a physical therapist who choose to use hippotherapy as a treatment to help Susan regain balance after her leg was amputated at the knee. The patient's health records were transferred to the physical therapist, who reviewed them to ensure there were no apparent precautions or contraindications. Although Susan disclosed during her intake that something "bad" had happened to her while she was deployed, her mental health records were not requested by the physical therapist. The therapist assumed if Susan had mental health needs, they would be addressed in counseling.

Given her health conditions, the physical therapist determined Susan would benefit from working with a horse with high withers and a narrow back. During her second session, Susan was mounted astride the horse sitting on a pad with a surcingle, and the horse was led through a simple obstacle course. The movements encouraged Susan to practice shifting her weight and maintaining her balance. After 10 minutes, the physical therapist noticed Susan seemed distracted, unfocused, and uncomfortable. After the session Susan was not able to recall details of the session or comments the therapist made during the session.

1. Describe why Susan may have responded the way she did to the activity. What mental health-related issue(s) might the physical therapist have missed?

   _____

   _____

   _____

   _____

2. Why would it be appropriate for the physical therapist (providing hippotherapy) to request the release of additional mental health information in this case?

   _____

   _____

   _____

3. Describe why the physical therapist chose a horse with a narrow back and high withers, and address why the obstacle course activity might have been chosen. What unintended negative outcomes may have occurred because of these choices?

_____

_____

_____

_____

4. Based upon the patient's response to the activity, what actions should the physical therapist have taken both during the session and after the session?

_____

_____

_____

_____

Bob is a 53-year-old man who suffered a stroke a year ago and lost his job. Although more physically functional now than when he first started services, Bob still deals with cognitive issues, mood swings, and depression. Bob was referred to an occupational therapist who used hippotherapy and the farm milieu to help him rehabilitate physically to return to work.

After six months, the occupational therapist referred him to a licensed mental health professional who worked out of the same facility to help him address his mood swings and depression. Bob had grown very comfortable with the equine facility, coming once or twice a week, and sometimes stopping by at other times to bring carrots to his favorite horses. Bob reports feeling safe and comfortable with the professionals who treat him, sometimes suggesting he doesn't even feel like it is "therapy" any longer. Likewise, the professionals report feeling like Bob is "part of the family," and invite him to farm gatherings, share personal stories, and sometimes ask for his help with tasks around the farm.

Although Bob has been able to return to work, his job is not going well and during a staff meeting the licensed mental health professional suggested maybe he could do work around the facility so he could earn extra money and also practice his vocational skills in a supportive environment. The team agreed this was a good plan for Bob, and when Bob was presented with the idea, he was elated.

1. What ethical boundaries may have been violated in this case scenario?

_____

_____

_____

_____

2. Describe how the concept of authenticity play into these ethical violations.

_____

_____

_____

_____

3. What are some possible positive and negative outcomes to this scenario?

_____

_____

_____

_____

4. What would you have done differently in this scenario?

_____

_____

_____

_____

☐ Hands-On Activity: Observation

Description: One of the best ways to connect to nature and understand animals is to be present in the natural environment without actively influencing it, and observe what happens around you. Many times, the business of daily life and work stressors get in the way of quiet reflection and observation. This activity is designed to help readers slow down, connect to the natural world, and learn from their animal partners.

Amount of Time: 20 minutes.

Directions: Find a quiet area where you can sit outside and watch animals (horses or other animals). Make sure you are outside of their space (e.g. on the other side of the fence). Bring this workbook, your journal, and some colored markers.

First, settle into your space. Get comfortable and relaxed. Now, simply look, feel, hear, and smell. Allow yourself to take in your surroundings without judgement or actively thinking. Take a few deep breaths, set aside other thoughts, and become focused on the present moment. Once you feel present and attuned to your environment, begin the observational activity by considering the following:

1. Practice your body scan. How does your body feel as it relaxes into the natural environment?

_____

_____

_____

_____

2. Bring your attention to the natural surroundings. What do you notice? Consider your senses. How does being in nature and close to animals make you feel? Breathe deeply and allow your body to slow down.

_____

_____

_____

_____

3. Now shift your attention to the animals. What creatures can you see, smell, and/or hear? What are they doing? Notice how they interact with each other and the natural world.

_____

_____

_____

_____

4. Next, take out your markers and draw the experience in your journal. NOTE: This is not about creating a piece of art. This is about self-expression and engaging your right brain through the act of spontaneous creativity. Try not to think or judge—just place your pen on the paper and draw. This exercise may make you uncomfortable. However, doing something new that might be challenging or different is what we ask of our patients every session. Use the drawing activity both to experience this sensation, and to free yourself from the common constraints of logic, order, and perfectionism.

_____

_____

_____

_____

☐ Journal Entry

Use these questions as an opportunity to explore your own ideas, thoughts, feelings, and personal reflections.

1. What was it like to draw your experience of nature and animals? What did you learn from this process?

_____

_____

_____

_____

2. Describe your relationship with nature and animals (including horses). Do you imagine yourself as a part of the natural world, or separate from it?

_____

_____

_____

_____

3. How do you foster this relationship? Are you task-oriented when engaging with nature and animals? How often do you give yourself time to simply be without doing?

_____

_____

_____

_____

4. What growth opportunities (both professionally and personally) do you see for yourself related to the human-animal-nature relationship?

_____

_____

_____

_____

5. How might you use the hands-on activity from this chapter with patients?

_____

_____

_____

_____

☐ Resources

Books & Articles

Allen, K. (2003). Are pets a healthy pleasure? The influence of pets on blood pressure. *Current Directions in Psychological Science, 12*(6), 236–239. Retrieved from: http://journals.sagepub.com/doi/abs/10.1046/j.0963-7214.2003.01269.x

Beck, A.M., & Katcher, A. (1996). *Between pets and people: The importance of animal companionship.* LaFayette, IN: Purdue University Press.

Bekoff, M. (2014). *Rewilding our hearts: Building pathways of compassion and coexistence.* New York: New World Library.

Chamberlin, J.E. (2006). *Horse: How the horse has shaped civilizations.* New York: Bluebridge.

Chandler, C.K. (2017). *Animal-assisted therapy in counseling* (3rd edition). Routledge.

Coholic, D. (2010). *Arts activities for children and young people in need: Helping children to develop mindfulness, spiritual awareness and self-esteem.* London: Jessica Kingsley Publishers.

Cook, R. (2013). *Brown Pony Series: Book One: Introduction to hippotherapy.* CreateSpace Independent Publishing Platform.

Engel, B., & MacKinnon, J.R. (2007). *Enhancing human occupation through hippotherapy: A guide for occupational therapy.* Bethesda, MD: AOTA Press.

Fine, A. (2015). *Handbook on animal-assisted therapy: Foundations and guidelines for animal-assisted interventions* (4th edition). Cambridge, MA: Academic Press.

Hill, C. (2006). *How to think like a horse: Essential insights for understanding equine behavior and building an effective partnership with your horse.* North Adams, MA: Storey Publishing, LLC.

Howey, M.O. (1923). *The horse in magic and myth, 2002 edition.* Mineola, NY: Dover Publications.

Kellert, S.R., & Wilson, E.O. (1993). *The biophilia hypothesis.* Washington, DC: Island Press.

Kohonov, L. (2001). *The tao of equus.* Novato, CA: New World Library.

Kohonov, L. (2003). *Riding between the worlds.* Novato, CA: New World Library.

Louv, R. (2008). *Last child in the woods: Saving our children from nature-deficit disorder.* New York, NY: Algonquin Books.

Louv, R. (2012). *The nature principle: Reconnecting with life in a virtual age.* New York, NY: Algonquin Books.

McCormick, A.R., & McCormick, M.D. (1997). *Horse sense and the human heart.* Deerfield Beach, FL: Health Communications.

McCormick, A.R., McCormick, M.D., & McCormick, T.E. (2004). *Horses and the mystical path.* Novato, CA: New World Library.

McGreevy, P.D. (2012). *Equine behavior: A guide for veterinarians and equine scientists* (2nd edition). Saunders Ltd.

Parish-Plass, N. (2013). *Animal-assisted psychotherapy: Theory, issues, and practice.* LaFayette, IN: Purdue University Press.

Salotto, P. (2001). *Pet assisted therapy: A loving intervention and an emerging profession: Leading to a friendlier, healthier, and more peaceful world.* Norton, MA: D. J. Publications.

Scanlan, L. (1998). *Wild about Horses.* New York: HarperCollins.

Schoen, A.M. (2002). *Kindred spirits: How the remarkable bond between humans and animals can change the way we live* (Reprint edition). New York: Broadway Books.

Selhub, E.M., & Logan, A.C. (2012). *Your brain on nature.* San Francisco, CA: John Wiley & Sons.

Stewart, L. (April 5, 2017). *What is your pet telling you?* Retrieved from: www.youtube.com/watch?v=oTVlCnenYeE

Waring, G.H. (2007). *Horse behavior* (2nd edition). Norwich, NY: William Andrew.

Animal-Assisted Therapy Training and Education Programs

Animal Assisted Therapy Programs of Colorado www.animalassistedtherapyprograms.org/animal-assisted-therapy-professional-training/

Animal Behavioral Institute Animal-Assisted Therapy Certificate www.animaledu.com/Programs/Animal-Assisted-Therapy?d=1

International Institute for Animal Assisted Play Therapy http://risevanfleet.com/international/certification/
Oakland University Animal-Assisted Therapy Certificate https://oakland.edu/nursing/continuing-education/animalassistedtherapy/Pet Partners www.petpartner.org
University of Denver Animal-Assisted Therapy Social Work Certificate www.du.edu/socialwork/programs/oncampus/twoyear/certificates/aaswcertificate.html
University of New Hampshire http://training.unh.edu/animaltherapy
University of North Texas www.coe.unt.edu/consortium-animal-assisted-therapy
Zur Institute www.zurinstitute.com/certificateinanimalassistedtherapy.html

Human-Animal Bonding (or Interactions) Centers

American Veterinary Medical Association www.avma.org/KB/Resources/Reference/human-animal-bond/Pages/Human-Animal-Bond-AVMA.aspx
Human-Animal Bond Initiative Research Institute www.habri.org
International Association of Human-Animal Interaction Organizations www.iahaio.org
International Society for Anthrozoology (ISAZ) www.isaz.net/isaz/
Purdue University www.vet.purdue.edu/chab/
University of Denver Institute for Human-Animal Connection www.du.edu/humananimalconnection/
University of Missouri Research Center for Human-Animal Interaction http://rechai.missouri.edu/
University of Pennsylvania Center for Interaction of Animals & Society www.vet.upenn.edu/research/centers-initiatives/center/center-for-interaction-of-animals-society

Other Websites

American Hippotherapy Association www.americanhippotherapyassociation.org
Care Farming www.carefarminguk.org
Fiddlehead Care Farm http://fiddleheadcarefarm.com/
Gould Farm www.gouldfarm.org/
Green Chimneys www.greenchimneys.org/
Kindred Spirits Care Farm www.kindredspiritscarefarm.org/
Sanctuary One at Double Oak Farm http://sanctuaryone.org/about/
Speech in Motion Blog www.speechinmotion.com/blog/
University of Minnesota Center for Spirituality and Healing Nature-Based Therapeutics www.csh.umn.edu/education/focus-areas/nature-based-therapeutics
University of Minnesota Pet Away Stress and Worry www.bhs.umn.edu/services/wellness-paws.htm

2 Understanding Equine-Assisted Therapy

☐ Chapter Two Summary

Equine-assisted therapy broadly refers to any type of therapy or treatment that includes equine interactions, activities, or treatment strategies, and the equine milieu. Services are regulated by healthcare laws and provided by appropriately educated, trained, and credentialed (licensed or registered) healthcare professionals. These individuals act within their scope of practice, and focus on addressing the patient's clinical treatment goals. Patients (or their parents or legal guardians in specific cases) seek therapy as a treatment for physical or psychological illness or disability, and agree to the treatment by signing an informed consent and actively engaging in the treatment planning process.

Specific to equine-assisted therapy, typically physical therapists, occupational therapists, speech therapists, mental health professionals, nurses, and on some occasions, medical doctors, are the licensed healthcare professionals who most commonly provide some type of equine-assisted therapy. Each of these professions apply equine-assisted therapy differently, and should identify their profession within the context of equine-assisted therapy (i.e. "equine-assisted physical therapy," "equine-assisted occupational therapy," "equine-assisted speech therapy," or "equine-assisted mental health," etc.).

Although equine-assisted therapy is widely used by licensed healthcare professionals to treat a variety of health conditions, misunderstanding or misuse of terminology has led to ethical concerns related to patient care, scope of practice violations, and challenges with research.

The lines between therapy and non-therapy services are frequently blurred, as it represented in both research and practice. It is the legal and ethical responsibility of both licensed healthcare professionals and non-licensed paraprofessionals to clearly represent the services they offer, and understand the professional ethics, standards, and laws that govern healthcare practices.

The industry of equine-assisted activities and therapies (EAAT) is faced with taking important steps to clarify the differences in terminology use and support the separation of therapy and non-therapy services. All professionals can assist in this process by being as knowledgeable as possible, and remaining clearly within their own scope of practice. Membership associations and training organizations can greatly support this important process by educating non-licensed individuals about ethical and legal violations, and how to appropriately represent the services they offer.

☐ Key Concepts

- "Therapy" is a regulated and sanctioned form of healthcare and can only be provided by licensed healthcare professionals, or those with the appropriate training and education who are supervised by a licensed healthcare professional.
- "Equine-assisted therapy" is not a distinct or separate profession. Rather, professionals continue to practice whatever form of conventional healthcare they are licensed to provide—such as physical, occupational, and speech therapy, or psychology, counseling, social work, or marriage and family therapy—while incorporating horses and the farm milieu into the patient's treatment plan.
- Scope of practice laws and term and title protections are in place to protect patients from harm, and non-licensed professionals cannot legally use certain terms or offer certain services that are protected by such laws.
- Misrepresenting a non-therapy service as a therapy service used to "treat" serious physical or mental health conditions is a serious ethical and, in some cases, legal violation.
- Hippotherapy is not a stand-alone clinical service; rather, it refers to how occupational, physical, and speech therapists incorporate equine movement and the farm milieu in a patient's treatment plan.
- The term "hippotherapy" should not be used interchangeably with the terms "adaptive riding" or "therapeutic riding."
- Adaptive or "therapeutic" riding offers opportunities for people with disabilities to learn to ride horses, and focuses on teaching riding skills. It is provided by non-licensed, but specially trained, riding instructors. It is not a form of therapy and should not be used to treat medical or mental health conditions. Therefore, it should not be confused with a regulated healthcare service.
- Similarly, equine-assisted learning is an educational or self-growth approach and is not a form of therapy and should not be confused with a regulated healthcare service. As such, equine-assisted learning should not be used to "treat" mental health conditions like depression, anxiety, or trauma.

☐ Learning Objectives

1. Recognize key terms and apply an understanding of these terms to practical scenarios.
2. Differentiate between therapy and non-therapy services, and identify, compare, and contrast the different types of equine-assisted therapy.
3. Describe scope of practice law, and demonstrate an understanding of its use.

☐ Relevant Terminology

Adaptive Riding: Adaptive riding is a non-therapy skills-based service in which specially trained instructors teach horseback riding and horsemanship skills to students with disabilities or special needs.

Cerebral Palsy: Cerebral palsy refers to a group of neurological disorders that appear in infancy or early childhood and permanently affect body movement and muscle coordination.

Combat-Related PTSD: An informal way to identify the unique trauma experienced by combat veterans and active military personnel as a sub-set of post-traumatic stress disorder. The military also uses the term "combat/operational stress" to describe the possible mental and emotional reactions of military personnel facing dangerous situations.

Equine-Assisted Learning: Equine-assisted learning (EAL) is a non-therapy skills-based service that focuses on teaching life skills, social skills, communication skills, or leadership skills while facilitating personal growth and increased self-awareness through both mounted and non-mounted interactions with horses. Services are provided by educators, riding instructors, or life/professional development coaches.

Equine-Assisted Mental Health: A term used to describe any type of mental health service (psychology, counseling, psychotherapy, social work, etc.) that includes horses or the farm milieu. Mental health services are provided by professionals who have graduated from an accredited education program and are allowed by law to include mental health treatment as a part of their scope of practice. These licensed professionals may choose between a variety of different approaches (see below) when providing equine-assisted mental health. The term "equine-assisted mental health" is sometimes used synonymously with "equine-assisted psychotherapy."

Equine-Assisted Occupational Therapy: This term describes the inclusion of horses in an occupational therapy service. Occupational therapy addresses physical, psychological, and cognitive aspects of wellbeing. Occupational therapy is provided by professionals who have graduated from an accredited occupational therapy education program and are licensed to practice occupational therapy.

Equine-Assisted Physical, Occupational, and Speech Therapy: Different practice specializations in which licensed physical, occupational, and speech therapists bring patients to the farm and use equine and farm-based activities as treatment strategies to address clinical goals.

Equine-Assisted Physical Therapy: This term describes the inclusion of horses in a physical therapy service. Physical therapy uses treatment techniques to promote the ability to move, reduce pain, restore function, and prevent disability. Physical therapy is provided by professionals who have graduated from an accredited physical therapy education program and are licensed to practice physical therapy.

Equine-Assisted Speech Therapy: This term describes the inclusion of horses in a speech, language, or hearing therapy service. Speech-language pathologists treat speech, language, social communication, cognitive-communication, and swallowing disorders. Speech therapy is provided by professionals who have graduated from an accredited speech-language-hearing education program and are licensed to practice speech therapy.

Hippotherapy: Refers to how occupational, physical, and speech therapists incorporate equine movement and the farm milieu in a patient's treatment plan, using clinical reasoning in the purposeful manipulation of equine movement to engage sensory, neuromotor, and cognitive systems to achieve functional outcomes.

Horse Handler: A horse expert whose responsibility it is to lead and direct the horse during a therapy session.

Mental Health Professionals: This term includes the professions of counseling, psychotherapy, social work, and psychology.

Service: This word is used in a few different ways throughout this book. In some cases, "service" is used generically, as in "work that is done for others as an occupation or business," or "work done for others, usually for pay." However, in the case of licensed healthcare professionals, whatever profession they are licensed to provide is usually considered the service. For example, the service licensed physical therapists provide is physical therapy, not hippotherapy. For insurance billing purposes, licensed professionals are urged make this distinction.

Side Walker: An assistant who walks alongside the patient, providing support while the patient is mounted on top of a horse.

☐ Questions to Explore

Use information presented in *The Clinical Practice of Equine-Assisted Therapy: Including Horses in Human Healthcare*, the recommended resources provided in this chapter of the workbook, and your own knowledge and experience to reflect on the following questions.

1. What are the distinguishing factors that make a service "therapy"?

   _____

   _____

   _____

   _____

2. Describe the difference between a therapy service and a non-therapy service. Why it is important to differentiate between the two?

   _____

   _____

   _____

   _____

3. Describe the differences between hippotherapy, adaptive riding, equine-assisted learning, and equine-assisted mental health in your own words.

   _____

   _____

   _____

   _____

4. What are the four types of equine-assisted therapy?

   _____

   _____

   _____

   _____

5. Explain how hippotherapy is used differently by physical, occupational, and speech therapists.

_____

_____

_____

_____

6. Picture observing a therapy session and a non-therapy session, what factors would help you identify the two services?

_____

_____

_____

_____

7. Explain scope of practice, and give one example of acting within your scope of practice and one example of acting outside of your scope of practice.

_____

_____

_____

_____

☐ Practical Scenarios

Read the Scenarios and Answer the Following Questions.

1. A 10-year-old diagnosed with cerebral palsy is mounted on a horse who is tacked up in a Western saddle. The boy is steering the horse with reins attached to the horse's halter while the horse is also being led by a horse handler. There are other riders in the arena and some of them are assisted by side walkers. One staff member stands in the middle of the arena, providing instructions to the riders.

    What service or treatment type is this?

    a. Adaptive riding
    b. Hippotherapy
    c. Equine-assisted mental health
    d. Equine-assisted learning

    What key factors helped you to identify the service or treatment type?

    _____

    _____

    _____

    _____

2. A CEO of a large corporation is taught by a staff member how to approach a loose horse in a small pen, and how to ask the horse to walk with him. The staff member then stands outside of the fence, observing the man practice this skill. After the man is finished with the activity, the staff member asks him how he will implement what he learned while managing members of his leadership team.

    What service or treatment type is this?

    a. Adaptive riding
    b. Hippotherapy
    c. Equine-assisted mental health
    d. Equine-assisted learning

    What key factors helped you to identify the service or treatment type?

    _____

    _____

    _____

    _____

3. A 10-year-old diagnosed with cerebral palsy is mounted astride a horse on a pad secured with a vaulting surcingle. He is sitting backwards, supported by two side walkers. A horse handler is leading the horse. There is a staff member near him, guiding him through various stretches and exercises. He and his team are the only ones in the arena.

What service or treatment type is this?

    a. Adaptive riding
    b. Hippotherapy
    c. Equine-assisted mental health
    d. Equine-assisted learning

What key factors helped you to identify the service or treatment type?

_____

_____

_____

_____

4. An 8-year-old diagnosed with a learning disability is practicing her math skills by coloring horse hooves on a chart, and adding up all the feet. Once she has completed the worksheet, the staff member leads her and others in her class over to the arena, where they observe loose horses and practice arithmetic by adding all the feet they can observe together (e.g. "there are five horses loose in the area. If each horse has four feet, how many feet are in the arena right now?").

What service or treatment type is this?

    a. Adaptive riding
    b. Hippotherapy
    c. Equine-assisted mental health
    d. Equine-assisted learning

What key factors helped you to identify the service or treatment type?

_____

_____

_____

_____

5. A 44-year-old woman sits by the fence observing the horses who are loose together in a pasture environment. She reflects that one of the mares reminds her of herself, mentioning how timid the mare seems to be, allowing other horses to push her around. The staff member sitting next to her asks, "Can you tell me what it feels like watching this happen?" The woman responds, noting it makes her feel badly about herself, sharing that her husband is aggressive and pushy with her, causing her to feel afraid to stand up for herself.

What service is this or treatment type?

   a. Adaptive riding
   b. Hippotherapy
   c. Equine-assisted mental health
   d. Equine-assisted learning

What key factors helped you to identify the service or treatment type?

_____

_____

_____

_____

6. A 30-year-old returning veteran is referred to a local equine-assisted psychotherapy program. The therapist has no additional training working with returning veterans, and has little experience dealing with combat-related PTSD. But she is excited to be able to help, especially after hearing how effective working with horses is for veterans, and accepts the patient immediately.

   a. Describe how this therapist is acting outside of her scope of practice.

_____

_____

_____

_____

   b. What would the therapist need to do to see this patient ethically and legally?

_____

_____

_____

_____

7. A licensed physical therapist who offers hippotherapy comes across an advertisement for a local adaptive riding program that states the services it offers "treats" a variety of health-related conditions, citing goals such as increased muscle tone, balance, and flexibility.

    a. What is the ethical concern presented in this case scenario?

_____

_____

_____

_____

    b. How might the licensed therapist address this concern?

_____

_____

_____

_____

☐ Hands-On Exercise: Professional Interview Activity

Locate one licensed professional who provides equine-assisted therapy from each of the four professions that most commonly include horses (physical therapy, occupational therapy, speech therapy, and mental health services) to interview about the unique differences and areas of possible overlap between the distinct professions.

Use the following questions for all four interviews and compare responses.

1. What type of equine-assisted therapy do you provide (e.g. equine-assisted physical therapy, equine-assisted occupational therapy, equine-assisted speech therapy, or equine-assisted mental health)?

_____

_____

_____

_____

2. What are the defining characteristics of this type of equine-assisted therapy? Include scope of practice, treatment goals addressed, treatment activities utilized, the role of the horse, and the role of the therapist.

_____

_____

_____

_____

3. What populations or conditions do you treat using equine-assisted therapy?

_____

_____

_____

_____

4. How is the type of therapy you offer different from a non-therapy service like adaptive riding or equine-assisted learning?

_____

_____

_____

_____

5. Do you find that you refer out to other providers of equine-assisted therapy? If so, what type of providers? It not, why?

_____

_____

_____

_____

☐ Journal Entry

Use these questions as an opportunity to explore your own ideas, thoughts, feelings, and personal reflections.

1. What was it like interviewing professionals in the industry? What did you learn from this activity? How will this information help you in the future?

_____

_____

_____

_____

2. Discussions about separating therapy from non-therapy services can be heated and emotional, as the topic is both financial and personal. What are your thoughts, feelings, and reactions?

_____

_____

_____

_____

3. How could you personally help to clarify the differences between therapy and non-therapy services, and use terminology that supports this effort?

_____

_____

_____

_____

☐ **Resources**

Books & Articles

American Counseling Association (ACA). (2016). *ACA Code of Ethics*. Retrieved from: www.counseling.org/resources/aca-code-of-ethics.pdf

American Hippotherapy Association (AHA). (2017). *AHA, Inc. Terminology*. Retrieved from: www.american hippotherapyassociation.org/wp-content/uploads/2015/02/Final-AHA-Terminology-Paper-3-9-2017.pdf

American Occupational Therapy Association (AOTA). (2016). *Occupational Therapy Code of Ethics, 2015*. Retrieved from: www.aota.org/-/media/corporate/files/practice/ethics/code-of-ethics.pdf

American Physical Therapy Association (APTA). (2015). *Code of Ethics for a Physical Therapist*. Retrieved from: www.apta.org/uploadedFiles/APTAorg/About_Us/Policies/Ethics/CodeofEthics.pdf

American Physical Therapy Association (APTA). (2016a). *The Physical Therapist Scope of Practice*. Retrieved from: www.apta.org/ScopeOfPractice/

American Physical Therapy Association (APTA). (2016b). *Term and Title Protection*. Retrieved from: www.apta.org/TermProtection/

American Psychological Association (APA). (2016). *Ethical Principles of Psychologists and Code of Conduct*. Retrieved from: www.apa.org/ethics/code/

American Speech-Language-Hearing Association (ASHA). (2016). *Code of Ethics*. Retrieved from: www.asha.org/Code-of-Ethics/

Cook, R. (2013). *Brown Pony Series: Book One: Introduction to hippotherapy*. CreateSpace Independent Publishing Platform.

Engel, B., & MacKinnon, J.R. (2007). *Enhancing human occupation through hippotherapy: A guide for occupational therapy*. Bethesda, MD: AOTA Press.

Hallberg, L. (2008). *Walking the way of the horse: Exploring the power of the horse-human relationship*. iUniverse.

National Association of Social Workers (NASW). (2016). *Code of Ethics of the National Association of Social Workers*. Retrieved from: www.socialworkers.org/pubs/Code/code.asp

National Board for Certified Counselors (NBCC). (2016). *Understanding National Certification and State Licensure*. Retrieved from: www.nbcc.org/Certification/CertificationorLicensure

Rutherford, M. (2008). Standardized nursing language: What does it mean for nursing practice? *Online Journal of Issues in Nursing*, *13*(1), 1–7. Retrieved from: www.nursingworld.org/MainMenuCategories/ThePracticeofProfessional Nursing/Health-IT/StandardizedNursingLanguage.html

Scott, N. (2005). *Special needs, special horses: A guide to the benefits of therapeutic riding*. Denton, TX: University of North Texas Press.

Spink, J. (1993). *Developmental riding therapy*. Communication Skill Builders.

Websites

American Counseling Association (ACA) www.counseling.org

American Hippotherapy Association (AHA) www.americanhippotherapyassociation.org

American Occupational Therapy Association (AOTA) www.aota.org

American Physical Therapy Association (APTA) www.apta.org

American Psychological Association (APA) www.apa.org

American Speech-Language-Hearing Association (ASHA) www.asha.org

National Association of Social Workers (NASW) www.socialworkers.org

National Board for Certified Counselors (NBCC) www.nbcc.org

Professional Association of Therapeutic Horsemanship, International (PATH Intl.) www.pathintl.org

Speech in Motion Blog www.speechinmotion.com/blog/

3 Professional Competencies in Equine-Assisted Therapy

☐ Chapter Three Summary

Providing equine-assisted therapy is a nuanced specialty. Appropriating another species to work in a human healthcare setting necessitates an additional level of training and education, both to protect the animal and the patient, and to safely and ethically provide the service.

Working with horses is considered inherently dangerous in 47 states in the United States. In order to safely and ethically provide equine-assisted therapy, licensed professionals should have in-depth horse knowledge, understand how to work with horses safely and respectfully, and utilize risk management strategies that will help to reduce the added risk of including horses in a healthcare service.

Licensed professionals who include an emerging treatment or specialty area of practice like equine-assisted therapy are ethically responsible for obtaining additional education and training to become competent in this new area. At present, various associations offer some guidance in regards to core competencies, most notably the American Hippotherapy Certification Board, the Certification Board for Equine Interaction Professionals, and the American Counseling Association.

Many training organizations also exist that offer a certificate of completion, which is not to be confused with a credentialing process. In some cases, when professionals are "certified" in a specific model of equine-assisted therapy, the public may misinterpret this as mastery at a credentialing level, or the equivalent of a professional license.

There are also a number of professional membership associations that provide support and resources for their members. Licensed healthcare professionals are urged to understand the differences between the various associations and organizations.

☐ Key Concepts

- Equine-assisted therapy is much more involved than simply owning and/or loving horses, and necessitates specialty education, training, and experience.
- There are many different ways to provide equine-assisted therapy. No single method or approach is right for every patient all the time. Professionals should be wary of any organization or individual that claims their approach is the "best" or "only" way to provide equine-assisted therapy.
- Therapists are ethically responsible for ensuring the safety and wellbeing of both the horses they work with and the patients they treat. Therapists must be able to gauge both the animal's response and the patient's, and alter services or activities based upon this information.

- Ethically and legally, the licensed healthcare professional is responsible for the clinical service, including using clinical reasoning to determine appropriate treatment activities, ensuring patient safety and confidentiality, and protecting the dignity of the patient at all times, and cannot abdicate these responsibilities to another party.
- Not every patient is suited for equine-assisted therapy. The inherent risks and additional cost and time commitment make it essential that therapists carefully and ethically select which patients to treat using equine-assisted therapy.
- Even if a patient appears appropriate for equine-assisted therapy, at any time during treatment he or she may need to be transferred back to an office setting.
- Therapists should be aware of their personal biases, including their own enjoyment of the outdoor setting or their love of horses, which may prompt them to make treatment decisions. It is important that therapists demonstrate clinical reasoning when deciding to provide equine-assisted therapy rather than make decisions based upon their own desires or biases.
- Training and certificate programs should not be confused with a formal credentialing process.

☐ Learning Objectives

1. Identify key areas of equine-assisted therapy competency.
2. Identify ethical and legal considerations related to competency in equine-assisted therapy.
3. Differentiate between training, a certificate of completion, and a credentialing process.
4. Analyze personal levels of competency in the various areas.

☐ Relevant Terminology

Certificate of Completion: A certificate of completion results from someone successfully completing a training or educational opportunity. Certificates of completion may be awarded for any type of training or educational event. Obtaining a certificate of completion does not validate overall competency, nor does it suggest that a professional is broadly qualified.

Clinically Indicated: When empirical evidence, practice patterns, and the careful clinical assessment of the patient appears to support the use of a procedure or treatment strategy.

Competence or Competency: The state or quality of being well-qualified and demonstrating a specific set of skills, knowledge, and ability.

Credential or Credentialing Process: Credentialing is a non-biased, non-methodologically specific process by which a third party validates the qualifications and competencies of a professional. Credentialing requires certain levels of education and experience, and competency is usually assessed by an exam. Credentialing bodies do not provide education or training.

Inherent Risk or Inherently Dangerous: Inherent risk or an activity that is "inherently dangerous" indicates there is natural and actual risk as opposed to "perceived risk," in which the danger is not real, but the individual participating in the activity is urged to act as if it were. For example, during a low ropes course initiative the participants may be told there is burning hot lava underneath a pole laid upon the ground that the group must walk across. Obviously there is no lava, and thus no actual risk associated with the activity, but the participants engage as if the risk were real.

Novel or Emerging Treatment: A type of treatment is that is new and generally not yet supported by conclusive empirical evidence.

Risk Management: The identification, assessment, and prioritization of risks. Usually, risk management includes strategies like writing policies, procedures, or protocols used to address existing risks and training staff.

Scope of Practice: The procedures, actions, and processes a healthcare professional is allowed to engage in under their licensure, and within state and federal law.

Specialty Area of Practice: Specializations of an existing profession that require additional training, education, experience, and supervision.

☐ Questions to Explore

Use information presented in *The Clinical Practice of Equine-Assisted Therapy: Including Horses in Human Healthcare*, the recommended resources provided in this chapter of the workbook, and your own knowledge and experience to reflect on the following questions.

1. Why is it important to receive specialty training and education in equine-assisted therapy?

    _____

    _____

    _____

    _____

2. After reading Chapter Three and reviewing the competency recommendations provided by the various organizations, identify core areas of competency for professionals interested in providing equine-assisted therapy.

    _____

    _____

    _____

    _____

3. Explain why including personal competencies like self-awareness, authenticity, and collaboration is an important a part of equine-assisted therapy training for professionals.

    _____

    _____

    _____

    _____

4. Describe the inherent ethical and legal challenges that exist if therapists are not trained to understand horse behavior, psychology, and physiology, or do not understand how to design or facilitate equine activities to meet clinical goals.

    _____

    _____

    _____

    _____

5. Why is training patients to understand equine communication, behavior, psychology, and physiology considered an essential risk management strategy?

_____

_____

_____

_____

6. What legal and ethical factors should a therapist consider before abdicating responsibility for the horse-related aspects of an equine-assisted therapy session to a non-licensed "horse professional"?

_____

_____

_____

_____

7. What legal and ethical factors should a therapist consider before asking any type of non-licensed staff, interns, or volunteers to be present during a clinical session?

_____

_____

_____

_____

8. Discuss the important components to include in a risk management plan for equine-assisted therapy.

_____

_____

_____

_____

9. Identify the differences between a credentialing process and a certificate of completion. Why is it important to differentiate between the two? What legal or ethical issues may be present if the public isn't made aware of these differences?

_____

_____

_____

_____

10. What is the purpose of a membership association? What are the differences between membership associations, credentialing bodies, and training organizations? Why are all three important?

_____

_____

_____

_____

11. Why is it OK for there to be multiple training organizations but limited membership associations and credentialing bodies?

_____

_____

_____

_____

☐ Practical Scenarios

Read the Scenarios and Answer the Following Questions.

Beth is a licensed mental health professional who owns her own horses. Although she has been a pleasure rider for years, she hasn't had any formal education or training about horses or about equine-assisted therapy. Beth read about equine-assisted mental health in a professional publication, and it sparked her attention. She decided to attend a three-day workshop to learn more. The workshop covered information about a specific approach or method to providing equine-assisted therapy. Beth learned some activities she could do with her patients, but little was discussed about the use of clinical reasoning when choosing between different activities or models. Also, the workshop did not include a focus on specific equine skills related to equine-assisted mental health, including learning to evaluate horses for signs of stress or burnout. But, since Beth loves her horses and has been taking care of them for years, she felt her knowledge was adequate. Beth assumed she would marry her counseling approach and theoretical knowledge with her love of horses, adding a few new equine-assisted mental health specific activities she could use with patients.

1. What ethical concerns are presented in this case study?

_____

_____

_____

_____

2. Does Beth's personal knowledge of horses transfer to equine-assisted mental health? Why or why not?

_____

_____

_____

_____

3. Does Beth need to adjunct her counseling knowledge and approach with additional specialty training specific to equine-assisted therapy? Why or why not?

_____

_____

_____

_____

Susan is an occupational therapist who offers hippotherapy at a local adaptive riding center. She is credentialed as a hippotherapy clinical specialist through the American Hippotherapy Certification Board. Since Susan's sessions take place at an adaptive riding center, it is possible for parents and other participants to see and sometimes hear what is occurring during Susan's sessions. She also uses the standard practice of including volunteer side walkers and horse handlers, and in many cases, the parents of her patients observe the session in the outdoor viewing area adjacent to the area.

Although occupational therapists like Susan have a distinctly different scope of practice than do physical therapists or speech therapists, which includes mental health services, Susan's training and certification for hippotherapy is the same as these other professionals. Therefore, it is common to see Susan using the same protocols and activity types even when she is addressing mental health-related goals.

1. What ethical considerations are presented in this case scenario?

_____

_____

_____

_____

2. How might Susan's scope of practice effect how or where she offers equine-assisted therapy?

_____

_____

_____

_____

3. How might Susan adapt her hippotherapy services to address these potential ethical considerations?

_____

_____

_____

_____

☐ Professional Competencies Self-Assessment

As providers of a novel treatment or specialty area of practice in an area without established competency standards or competency assessment protocols, objectively evaluating one's own competency is an essential activity. This assessment is meant for your eyes only, although you may use the results to help guide your acquisition of knowledge, or you may discuss the results with a mentor or supervisor. Try not to be judgmental of your responses and be as honest and authentic as possible. This is meant to be a tool for you to use as you continue to grow and learn as a professional.

Use the following system to rank your level of professional competency—The higher the total score, the more competent you view yourself in that area.

_____ **1**= Beginner or novice (minimal experience, lacking expertise)
_____ **2**= Intermediate (1–5 years of experience, currently developing expertise through specialty education and training)
_____ **3**= Advanced (5+ years of extensive experience with past specialty education and training)
_____ **4**= Expert (10+ years of experience, university-level education, and past specialty education and training)

Horse Knowledge

_____ Identify equine anatomy and physiology.
_____ Recognize equine communication (ears, facial features, feet, tail, vocal communications) and accurately interpret meaning.
_____ Explain equine psychology, learning, and behavior using equitation science, behavior science, and equine ethology academic resources.
_____ Recognize behaviors associated with herd dynamics and social hierarchy.
_____ Identify equine gates and confirmation flaws.
_____ Describe the desirable qualities of the horse's movement as a possible agent of change.
_____ Identify equine breeds, colors, and markings, and describe breed characteristics.
_____ Identify common equine aliments (lameness, colic, laminitis, strangles, cushings, rain rot).
_____ Take vitals.
_____ Recognize signs of pain or illness.
_____ Recognize signs of depression, anxiety, fear, or burnout.
_____ Identify recognized standards for equine care and welfare.
_____ Identify key elements of an equine's physical environment that affect its quality of care.
_____ Describe what is typically included in customary best practices for equine care.
_____ Describe equine selection criteria for specific types of equine-assisted therapy.
_____ **TOTAL SCORE**

Horse Skills

_____ Approaching and moving around loose or stalled horses.
_____ Haltering.
_____ Leading.
_____ Tying (ground tie, cross ties, tying to a fixed point, proper rope length, knots).

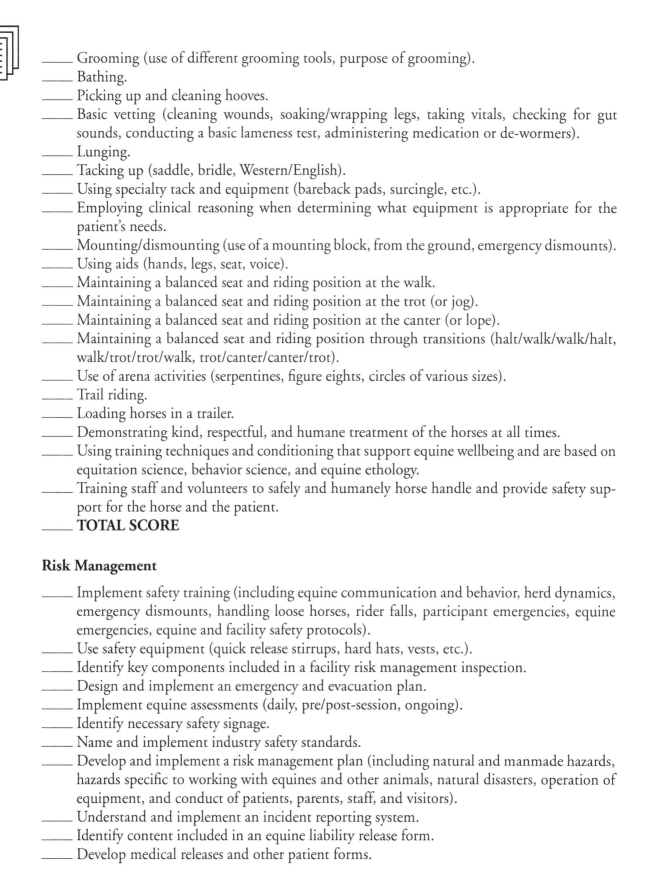

_____ Grooming (use of different grooming tools, purpose of grooming).

_____ Bathing.

_____ Picking up and cleaning hooves.

_____ Basic vetting (cleaning wounds, soaking/wrapping legs, taking vitals, checking for gut sounds, conducting a basic lameness test, administering medication or de-wormers).

_____ Lunging.

_____ Tacking up (saddle, bridle, Western/English).

_____ Using specialty tack and equipment (bareback pads, surcingle, etc.).

_____ Employing clinical reasoning when determining what equipment is appropriate for the patient's needs.

_____ Mounting/dismounting (use of a mounting block, from the ground, emergency dismounts).

_____ Using aids (hands, legs, seat, voice).

_____ Maintaining a balanced seat and riding position at the walk.

_____ Maintaining a balanced seat and riding position at the trot (or jog).

_____ Maintaining a balanced seat and riding position at the canter (or lope).

_____ Maintaining a balanced seat and riding position through transitions (halt/walk/walk/halt, walk/trot/trot/walk, trot/canter/canter/trot).

_____ Use of arena activities (serpentines, figure eights, circles of various sizes).

_____ Trail riding.

_____ Loading horses in a trailer.

_____ Demonstrating kind, respectful, and humane treatment of the horses at all times.

_____ Using training techniques and conditioning that support equine wellbeing and are based on equitation science, behavior science, and equine ethology.

_____ Training staff and volunteers to safely and humanely horse handle and provide safety support for the horse and the patient.

_____ **TOTAL SCORE**

Risk Management

_____ Implement safety training (including equine communication and behavior, herd dynamics, emergency dismounts, handling loose horses, rider falls, participant emergencies, equine emergencies, equine and facility safety protocols).

_____ Use safety equipment (quick release stirrups, hard hats, vests, etc.).

_____ Identify key components included in a facility risk management inspection.

_____ Design and implement an emergency and evacuation plan.

_____ Implement equine assessments (daily, pre/post-session, ongoing).

_____ Identify necessary safety signage.

_____ Name and implement industry safety standards.

_____ Develop and implement a risk management plan (including natural and manmade hazards, hazards specific to working with equines and other animals, natural disasters, operation of equipment, and conduct of patients, parents, staff, and visitors).

_____ Understand and implement an incident reporting system.

_____ Identify content included in an equine liability release form.

_____ Develop medical releases and other patient forms.

_____ Identify content included in an informed consent for treatment.

_____ Understand patient confidentiality laws and ethics, and implement practices to protect patient confidentiality.

_____ Understand and implement HIPAA requirements.

_____ Identify equine liability insurance requirements.

_____ Understand equine-assisted therapy precautions and contraindications related to various populations or conditions.

_____ **TOTAL SCORE**

Equine-Assisted Therapy Specific Knowledge

_____ Identify foundational theories used when conducting equine-assisted therapy (include theories related to human-animal bonding, nature-based therapies, and theories of change).

_____ Distinguish between therapy services and non-therapy services.

_____ Identify different types of equine-assisted therapy services.

_____ Identify the role of the horse in the specific type of equine-assisted therapy provided (e.g. what theory will be utilized to explain or validate the inclusion of a horse in therapy?).

_____ Identify the other staff members or volunteers who will be present during an equine-assisted therapy session, define their roles, and implement protocols to protect patient confidentiality.

_____ Use an assessment, evaluation, and intake process to determine which patients are appropriate for equine-assisted therapy, taking into consideration possible precautions and contraindications.

_____ Demonstrate intentionality and clinical reasoning to support the use of equine-assisted therapy when writing treatment plans, treatment goals, and designing treatment activities.

_____ Match equine-assisted activities to clinical treatment goals using a variety of activity types.

_____ Identify which treatment approach of equine-assisted therapy is most appropriate for different populations or conditions (hippotherapy, equine-facilitated psychotherapy, the EAGALA model of equine-assisted psychotherapy, etc.), and demonstrate the ability to justify this decision using clinical reasoning.

_____ If mounted work is used, describe how the horse's movement impacts human systems, what positions might be most effective for various conditions, how the patient may respond to equine movement and mounted positioning, and the associated precautions and contraindications.

_____ Identify and implement ethical standards of practice.

_____ Identify and implement scope of practice laws and ethics.

_____ Facilitate equine-assisted therapy activities to meet clinical goals.

_____ Set up a session plan (what activity, how long it will take, equipment needed, staff needed, appropriate horse, facility considerations).

_____ Train staff and volunteers to perform their jobs effectively.

_____ Use pre/post-objective measures to identify treatment outcomes.

_____ Choose horses and other animal partners and the setting the session will take place based upon clinical reasoning and the patient's needs and treatment goals.

_____ Evaluate the facility for clinical appropriateness.

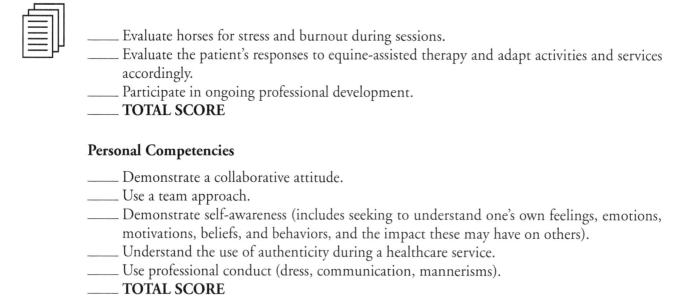

_____ Evaluate horses for stress and burnout during sessions.

_____ Evaluate the patient's responses to equine-assisted therapy and adapt activities and services accordingly.

_____ Participate in ongoing professional development.

_____ **TOTAL SCORE**

Personal Competencies

_____ Demonstrate a collaborative attitude.

_____ Use a team approach.

_____ Demonstrate self-awareness (includes seeking to understand one's own feelings, emotions, motivations, beliefs, and behaviors, and the impact these may have on others).

_____ Understand the use of authenticity during a healthcare service.

_____ Use professional conduct (dress, communication, mannerisms).

_____ **TOTAL SCORE**

_____ **TOTAL SELF-ASSESSMENT SCORE**

☐ Hands-On Activity: Safety Talk

Description: Educating and training people about horses is one of the most effective risk management strategies available to providers of equine-assisted therapy. Learning about equine psychology, physiology, behavior, and communication can help patients, staff, and volunteers better understand and more safely respond to horses.

Amount of Time: 20 minutes (to present the safety talk).

Directions: Develop and practice your own safety talk that covers the following topics:

- Equine communication (including ears, facial expressions, feet and legs, tails, and vocalizations) and how the patient should react and respond.
- Basic introduction to equine physiology, psychology, and senses (how horses see, hear, smell, and touch).
- Herd dynamics and social hierarchy (if working with loose horses).
- How to stay safe around both loose and restrained horses (including approaching, moving around, touching).
- Other safety protocols including anything specific to the facility or individual animals.

☐ **Journal Entry**

Use these questions as an opportunity to explore your own ideas, thoughts, feelings, and personal reflections.

1. Generally, what did you learn about competency and equine-assisted therapy from reading this Chapter Three?

_____

_____

_____

_____

2. What did you learn from taking the competency self-assessment? What goals might you set for yourself as a result?

_____

_____

_____

_____

3. How do you think using a safety talk to help educate your patients, staff, and volunteers about horses can help reduce risk? How do you think using this safety talk can also help the horses?

_____

_____

_____

_____

☐ **Resources**

Books & Articles

American Counseling Association (ACA). (2016). *Animal-Assisted Therapy in Counseling Competencies*. Retrieved from: www.counseling.org/docs/default-source/competencies/animal-assisted-therapy-competencies-june-2016.pdf?sfvrsn=14

American Hippotherapy Certification Board (AHCB). *Exams and Certification*. Retrieved from: http://hippotherapycertification.org/exams-and-certification/

Certification Board for Equine Interaction Professionals (CBEIP). (2016). *CBEIP Certification Workbook*. Retrieved from: www.cbeip.org/mental-health-exam

Cook, R. (2014). *Risk management and safety in hippotherapy*. Publisher: Rebecca Cook.

Cook, R. (2015). *Brown Pony Series: Book Three: Considering hippotherapy in your career plans*. CreateSpace Independent Publishing Platform.

Hill, C. (2006). *How to think like a horse: Essential insights for understanding equine behavior and building an effective partnership with your horse*. North Adams, MA: Storey Publishing, LLC.

Institute for Credentialing Excellence (ICE). (2016). *What Is Credentialing?* Retrieved from: www.credentialingexcellence.org/p/cm/ld/fid=32

Matthews, J.H. (2012). Role of professional organizations in advocating for the nursing profession. *Online Journal of Issues in Nursing*, *17*(1), 1–10. Retrieved from: http://nursingworld.org/MainMenuCategories/ANAMarketplace/ANAPeriodicals/OJIN/TableofContents/Vol-17-2012/No1-Jan-2012/Professional-Organizations-and-Advocating.html

McDonnell, S. (2003). *The equid ethogram: A practical field guide to horse behavior*. Lexington, KY: Eclipse Press.

McDonnell, S. (2005). *Understanding your horse's behavior*. Lexington, KY: Eclipse Press.

McGreevy, P. (2012). *Equine behavior: A guide for veterinarians and equine scientists* (2nd edition). Philadelphia, PA: Saunders Ltd.

McGreevy, P., & McLean, A. (2010). *Equitation science*. Hoboken, NJ: Wiley-Blackwell.

National Environmental Health Association (NEHA). (2016). *Difference between Credentials and Certifications*. Retrieved from: www.neha.org/professional-development/education-and-training/differences-between-credentials-certifications

Schoen, A., & Gordon, S. (2015). *The compassionate equestrian: 25 principles to live by when caring for and working with horses*. North Pomfret, VT: Trafalgar Square Books.

Walker, A., Yong, M., Pang, L., Fullarton, C., Costa, B., & Dunning, A.M.T. (2013). Work readiness of graduate health professionals. *Nurse Education Today*, *33*(2), 116–122. Retrieved from: www.researchgate.net/publication/221834283_Work_readiness_of_graduate_health_professionals

Waring, G.H. (2007). *Horse behavior* (2nd edition). Norwich, NY: William Andrew.

U.S. Equine-Assisted Activities or Therapies College Programs

Arkansas State University www.astate.edu/college/conhp/centers-clinics-programs/

Ashbury University www.asbury.edu/academics/departments/psychology/equine-facilitated-wellness

Bethany College www.bethanywv.edu/academics/departments/biology/equine-studies-pro/minors/

Carroll College www.carroll.edu/academic-programs/anthrozoology

Colorado State University http://tgec.agsci.colostate.edu/

North Dakota State University www.ag.ndsu.edu/equinescience/undergraduate-programs-1/therapeutic-horsemanship

Ohio University Southern www.ohio.edu/southern/health/therapeutic-riding/

Prescott College www.prescott.edu/academics/concentrations/equine-assisted-mental-health

Rocky Mountain College www.rocky.edu/academics/academic-programs/undergraduate-majors/equine/TherapeuticRiding.php

Santa Rosa Junior College https://ag.santarosa.edu/equine-science

St. Mary-of-the-Woods www.smwc.edu/academic/social-and-behavioral-sciences/equine-assisted-therapy/
SUNY Cobleskill www.cobleskill.edu/academics/schools/agriculture-and-natural-resources/animal-science/therapeutic-
   horsemanship.asp
Texas Tech University www.afs.ttu.edu/ttrc
University of Denver www.du.edu/humananimalconnection/programs-education/eamh.html
University of New Hampshire www.trp.unh.edu
University of Wisconsin River Falls www.uwrf.edu/ANFS/EquineEmphasis.cfm
Utah State University https://extension.usu.edu/equine/equine-therapy
Virginia Intermont College www.vic.edu/learn/majors/equine-studies/
Waubonsee Community College www.waubonsee.edu/learning/personalProfessional/workforce/professional/
   therapeuticRidingInstr/
West Virginia University https://horses.wvu.edu/

Equine-Assisted Therapy Training and/or Certificate Programs

Adventures in Awareness (AIA) www.adventuresinawareness.net
American Hippotherapy Association, Inc. (AHA) www.americanhippotherapyassociation.org
Eponaquest www.eponaquest.com
Equine Assisted Growth and Learning Association (EAGALA) www.eagala.org
Equine Psychotherapy Institute www.equinepsychotherapy.net.au
Gestalt Equine Institute of the Rockies (GEIR) www.gestaltequineinstitute.com
High Hopes Therapeutic Riding http://highhopestr.org/learn/training-education/
Horse Sense of the Carolinas http://horsesenseotc.com/for-eap-professionals/
Human-Equine Alliances for Learning (HEAL) www.humanequinealliance.com
Human-Equine Relational Development Institute (HERD) www.herdinstitute.com
LEAP Equine www.leapequine.com/
Professional Association of Therapeutic Horsemanship, International (PATH Intl.) www.pathintl.org

4 Populations Served by Equine-Assisted Therapy

☐ Chapter Four Summary

Although widely popular and highly touted, equine-assisted therapy still lacks the conclusive empirical evidence needed to establish its efficacy. Benefit claims tend to be made based upon anecdotal reports, or upon the results of a few studies that show tentative support for the intervention.

Healthcare professionals who offer equine-assisted therapy tend to be very passionate about their work, sometimes mistakenly overstating the benefits or possible positive results. Challenges with research methodology and an industry-wide lack of consistent terminology and practice patterns have hampered effects to establish conclusive results. Additional confusion is caused by the tendency for researchers to combine and compare therapy services offered by licensed healthcare professionals to non-therapy services offered by non-licensed adaptive riding instructors, educators, or coaches. Many research projects investigate the use of a non-therapy service like adaptive riding or equine-assisted learning to treat serious physical and mental health-related conditions. This is likely to drastically alter or skew research results.

In many cases, researchers have focused primarily on projects that could help to establish the intervention as clinically efficacious, rather than seeking to understand the mechanisms of change that may be taking place. This has resulted in a general lack of understanding about equine-assisted therapy, even while the body of research continues to grow.

Since licensed professionals are ethically responsible for being knowledgeable about current research related to any intervention or service they provide, it is important for them to gain a more objective, and possibly less personally biased perspective. These professionals are urged to consider equine-assisted therapy as a "novel" treatment, one that necessitates more research, continued curiosity, and a deeper level of understanding.

☐ Key Concepts

- Many benefit claims are made about equine-assisted therapy. Most cannot be substantiated by the results of empirical research.
- Although there are currently 200+ research articles specific to populations or conditions served by an equine-assisted interaction and published in peer-reviewed journals, results are considered generally inconclusive due to methodological challenges.
- The industry does not need more poor-quality research focusing on efficacy. Rather, more high-quality research must be conducted to conclusively determine if equine-assisted therapy is an effective treatment for the various conditions and populations studied.

- The focus of equine-assisted therapy research should expand to include studies aimed at understanding the individual factors contributing to change, the possible negative effects of the treatment, and the impact of equine-assisted therapy on the horses.
- Systematic and literature reviews are helpful in establishing a sound basis for any clinical intervention. At present, 23 such reviews have been written documenting the various equine-assisted interventions studies, and highlighting the opportunities and challenges related to equine-assisted therapy research.
- The most well researched of all conditions addressed by an equine-assisted interaction at this time is cerebral palsy with a total of 42 current studies. This is followed by autism (24), "at-risk" youth (16), non-combat PTSD, trauma, and abuse (14), the elderly (10), psychiatric conditions or mental illness (10), stroke (eight), veterans and active military personnel (seven), multiple sclerosis (six), addictions and chemical dependency (five), eating disorders (four), other neurological conditions (four), prison populations (three), anxiety (three), Down syndrome (three), other intellectual disabilities (three), back pain (three), cancer (two), spinal cord injury (two), self-harm (two), and grief (two). An additional 25 papers were identified that could not be coded into any of those categories, as well as 13 papers related to non-clinical interventions and populations.

☐ Learning Objectives

1. Differentiate between empirical research and anecdotal evidence.
2. Identify current challenges with equine-assisted therapy research.
3. Describe the importance of separating therapy and non-therapy services.
4. Analyze personal biases, and describe how these biases might affect equine-assisted therapy research.

☐ Relevant Terminology

Control Group: The group in an experiment or study that does not receive the same treatment as the participants who are being studied. This group acts as a benchmark to measure treatment results against.

Equine-Assisted Interaction: This term is used to describe the wide range of services represented in published research articles that include both therapy and non-therapy services used to address physical and mental health-related conditions.

Evidence-Based Practice: Evidence-based practice refers to models, methods, or treatments that integrate the results of high quality research with clinical expertise, and take into consideration the patient's individual needs, beliefs, and values. Without all three of these areas in place, the practice is not considered evidence-based. The ideal outcome of an evidence-based practice is that the patient receives patient-centered services while also obtaining the best possible care for their condition as evidenced by current research.

Novel or Emerging Treatment: A new type of treatment that is still investigational in nature, and has yet to be empirically-proven.

Withers: Usually the tallest point of the horse's back, immediately before the neck begins. A rider sites immediately behind the withers.

☐ Questions to Explore

Use information presented in *The Clinical Practice of Equine-Assisted Therapy: Including Horses in Human Healthcare*, the recommended resources provided in this chapter of the workbook, and your own knowledge and experience to reflect on the following questions.

1. What is the difference between anecdotal reports and empirical evidence? Give an example of how an anecdotal report could potentially mislead the public. What are the ethical concerns?

   _____

   _____

   _____

   _____

2. What types of methodological issues plague equine-assisted interaction research? How do these issues impact research results?

   _____

   _____

   _____

   _____

3. Review the existing equine-assisted interaction research (go to www.leifhallberg.com for a comprehensive literature review). Notice what type of service was provided and by whom. Pay special attention to how many studies were conducted using a therapy approach rather than a non-therapy service. Discuss the ethical concerns of using a non-therapy approach to treat medical or mental health conditions. Also discuss issues of transferability. Can licensed professionals use the results of a research study to support their clinical work if the study used a non-therapy approach? Why or why not?

   _____

   _____

   _____

   _____

4. Why is separating therapy and non-therapy services important for research? How might combining the results of these very different services effect or skew research results?

_____

_____

_____

_____

5. As an equine-assisted therapy provider, how can you help to ensure patients and parents are presented with accurate information related to the benefits of equine-assisted therapy?

_____

_____

_____

_____

6. Describe why equine-assisted therapy is considered a novel treatment rather than an "evidenced-based practice".

_____

_____

_____

_____

7. What surprised you about this chapter? What did you learn? Discuss your own feelings, reactions, and possible personal biases related to research and equine-assisted therapy.

_____

_____

_____

_____

☐ **Practical Scenarios**

Read the Scenarios and Answer the Following Questions.

A local adaptive riding center also offers hippotherapy provided by a physical therapist. The website suggests research shows the following populations or conditions benefit from hippotherapy:

- Veterans
- Traumatic brain injuries
- Autism
- Cerebral palsy

1. Which of these populations or conditions have been empirically studied using hippotherapy?

   _____

   _____

   _____

   _____

2. To date, what equine-assisted interactions have been used in published research projects studying the benefits for veterans?

   _____

   _____

   _____

   _____

3. What are the potential ethical concerns of advertising benefits that cannot be substantiated by empirical evidence? What would you do to address these concerns if you were the physical therapist working at this center?

   _____

   _____

   _____

   _____

4. Describe another way to present possible positive outcomes that could come from interactions with horses.

_____

_____

_____

_____

A research project studies the effects of equine-assisted mental health on children with a history of sexual abuse. Sessions are conducted at the farm where children interact with horses and other farm animals, and participate in art and nature-based activities. The therapists use an eclectic therapeutic approach, combining aspects of Gestalt therapy and client-centered or humanistic therapy. The control group attends group trauma-focused cognitive behavioral therapy in an office setting and participants are taught emotional regulation skills, stress reduction techniques, and coping strategies.

1. What research methodology challenges are highlighted in this scenario?

_____

_____

_____

_____

2. How might these challenges impact research outcomes?

_____

_____

_____

_____

3. How could the research have been designed differently to avoid these challenges?

_____

_____

_____

_____

Mary, a licensed mental health professional, offers equine-assisted therapy and would like to contribute to the growing body of research. She serves "at-risk" children and adolescents, and believes that her equine-assisted therapy approach is effecting change in these individuals. Mary is excited to think that if the results of research show positive change, her work will be more substantiated, and thus she could receive additional funding for her services. Mary is not a trained researcher, but partners with a professional from a local university. Mary and the researcher develop protocol and an assessment tool to use before and after each equine-assisted therapy session. Mary conducts the sessions and administers the assessment.

1. What possible ethical concerns are presented in this case scenario?

_____

_____

_____

_____

2. What could Mary have done differently in this scenario?

_____

_____

_____

_____

☐ Biases and Beliefs Self-Assessment

This is the second of three times you will take this self-assessment. Do not go back and read your responses to the first self-assessment until you have completed this self-assessment. Try to be as honest and authentic as possible. Remember, this is meant for your eyes only, although you may choose to use some of your responses in supervision, or discuss with peers as you feel comfortable. Try not to be judgmental of your own responses, rather view this an opportunity to discover something new about yourself.

Rank the following statements accordingly: 1 = Strongly disagree, 2 = Disagree, 3 = Unsure or somewhere in the middle, 4 = Agree, 5 = Strongly agree. Total your score at the bottom of the self-assessment. A higher score indicates greater levels of acceptance, open-mindedness, and collaboration.

_____ I am open-minded and curious about how other people practice equine-assisted therapy.

_____ I research my beliefs, taking into consideration many different perspectives, and am comfortable changing my opinions based upon what I learn.

_____ I continually strive to learn more about equine-assisted therapy.

_____ I learn from other people's perspectives, and implement their ideas if applicable.

_____ I ask lots of questions and attempt to understand why other people think or believe the way they do.

_____ I see value in everyone's perspectives, and encourage open discussion about differences.

_____ I find collaboration refreshing, helpful, productive, and enjoyable.

_____ I enjoy and seek out collaborative environments or opportunities.

_____ I seek outside/expert support and guidance when making hard clinical decisions.

_____ I believe there are many different ways to work with horses, and I am open to trying new ideas.

_____ I seek outside/expert support and guidance when evaluating my horses' health and wellbeing.

_____ I take the advice of other people when it comes to addressing health and wellness issues with my horses.

_____ I make time to provide help and guidance to those new to the industry, and answer their questions with respect, patience, and open-mindedness.

_____ I welcome newcomers to the industry, and believe they have something to teach me.

_____ I am comfortable referring my patients to other professionals.

_____ When people ask me questions about equine-assisted therapy, I learn from their questions and find myself expanding my own knowledge because of their query.

_____ I make time to learn something new about equine-assisted therapy on a regular basis.

_____ I am easy to approach, and encourage conversation.

_____ I am less likely to judge people, and more likely to learn about them and their beliefs.

_____ I enjoy differences in beliefs and find those differences valuable.

_____ I commonly use peer or professional supervision as a way to check my own decisions and beliefs.

_____ I use scholarly resources such as text books or peer-reviewed journals to inform my opinions and guide my decision making.

_____ I ask the opinions of others and listen to their advice, implementing applicable information.

_____ I am not defensive about my clinical decisions and an open to critique and suggestions.

_____ I am not defensive about my horse care decisions and an open to critique and suggestions.

_____ I don't assume that equine-assisted therapy is right for every patient.

_____ I keep my personal beliefs about how horses might impact people out of the therapy process.

_____ I don't use equine-assisted therapy for every patient, and rather make careful choices about which patients would be best served by the treatment.

_____ I understand and value the investigative nature of equine-assisted therapy.

_____ I don't try to defend equine-assisted therapy as a "proven" clinical intervention, and if research results show less than positive effects, I am open and curious.

_____ I am able to separate my own love for horses from the clinical use of equine-assisted therapy.

_____ I provide equine-assisted therapy first because of the clinical benefits it offers the patient, and second because I enjoy it.

_____ I am open to the idea that working with another animal could produce similar health benefits as working with horses.

_____ I don't need my "way" of working with horses or providing equine-assisted therapy to be "right." I am open to many different approaches.

_____ I model collaborative values, believing this is important to teach patients as well as foster in other professionals.

_____ **TOTAL SCORE**

©2018, _The Equine-Assisted Therapy Workbook: A Learning Guide for Professionals and Students_, Leif Hallberg, Routledge

☐ Hands-On Activity: Meeting, Greeting, Moving Around

Description: One of the best ways to teach patients, staff, and volunteers how to be safe around horses is to invite them to engage with horses and get to know them through observation and introduction. Practice this activity yourself to develop different ways to lead the activity based upon populations and conditions.

Amount of Time: 20 minutes.

Directions: First, choose a setting that suits you and/or your clinical work. For example, an occupational therapist working with a child with an intellectual disability may want the horse held by a volunteer during this activity, whereas a licensed mental health professional working with an adult dealing with trauma might choose to work with loose horses in a pasture setting. Once the setting has been established, review the safety talk.

When considering this activity for clinical use, remember, *all parts of this activity can be adapted based upon patient functionality.* This activity can be conducted with patients of all levels of function, including those in wheelchairs or with speech and language difficulties. Be creative!

1. *Meeting:* Given the way horses see and respond, approaching the horse at the side is the safest and best way to begin. Practice moving smoothly and directly towards the horse, watching his/her ears for signs as to how the horse is receiving your approach. If the horse begins to put his/her ears back or moves away, Stop. This demonstrates respect and understanding of his/her communication. Remain where you are or even take a step back. Allow the horse to become curious and pursue investigation. Once the horse's ears are perked forwards or in the listening position, attempt your approach again. Repeat as many times as needed until the horse "invites" you in.

2. *Greeting:* Once you are close enough, reach your hand towards the horse's withers. Assuming the horse is still inviting, scratch or rub around the wither area. Try to avoid patting. Notice if the horse seems to like the physical touch, or moves away. If he/she moves away, try something different or stop touching altogether and just stand next to the horse. Remember, not all horses like to be touched, or may have specific ways they like to be touched. Allow the horse to investigate you with his/her nuzzle. This is an important step in getting to know each other and is not often allowed.

3. *Moving Around:* Once you have both investigated each other, practice moving around the horse. This is an important safety skill. When moving around a horse, you should keep your hand on the horse at all times. If you are going behind the horse, go as close as possible, keeping your hand on the horse as you move. Continue to keep your hand on the horse until you return to the other shoulder. If you need to move behind the horse when you aren't close, practice using the "elephant's distance" rule, which means you leave the horse's shoulder and walk "way, way, way around the horse" and begin the entire process of approaching again from the other side. NEVER approach the horse from the rear or without proper notice.

4. As you practice this activity, consider that research shows horses respond differently to nervous people. Teaching patients (and yourself) how to communicate feelings is a valuable skill, and can also help the horse by validating that his/her reactions might not reflect a behavioral issue, but rather something going on for the human.

5. Allowing patients (and yourself) to acknowledge feelings also could lead to slowing down activities. For instance, if the patient realizes he/she is actually quite nervous or fearful, an opportunity exists to take a step back and not push the patient into doing whatever it is that invokes those feelings. It may be that with additional time or more information, the patient will become less afraid and feel safe to continue.

☐ Journal Entry

Use these questions as an opportunity to explore your own ideas, thoughts, feelings, and personal reflections.

1. What did you learn about yourself while doing the hands-on activity? Did you notice any urge to rush through the "meeting" component of the hands-on activity? What did it feel like to practice slowing down, listening, and responding to the horse's communication?

_____

_____

_____

_____

2. How might you use this hands-on activity clinically with patients?

_____

_____

_____

_____

3. Were the results of your "Biases and Beliefs Self-Assessment" different this time, or the same? What reflections do you have about this?

_____

_____

_____

_____

4. How might your personal biases or beliefs effect how you interpret and use research results, or conduct research?

_____

_____

_____

_____

☐ **Resources**

Books & Articles

American Occupational Therapy Association (AOTA). (2017). *Evidence-Based Practice*. Retrieved from: www.aota. org/About-Occupational-Therapy/Professionals/EBP.aspx

American Psychological Association (APA). (2006). *Evidence-Based Practice in Psychology*. Retrieved from: www.apa. org/pubs/journals/features/evidence-based-statement.pdf

American Psychological Association (APA). (2009). *Publication manual of the American Psychological Association* (6th edition). Washington, DC: American Psychological Association.

American Speech-Language-Hearing Association (ASHA). *Introduction to Evidence-Based Practice: What It Is (And What It Isn't)*. Retrieved from: www.asha.org/Research/EBP/Introduction-to-Evidence-Based-Practice/

Barnard, C. (2007). Ethical regulation and animal science: Why animal behaviour is special. *Animal Behaviour*, *74*(1), 5–13. Retrieved from: http://doi.org/10.1016/j.anbehav.2007.04.002

Beck, A.M., & Katcher, A.H. (2003). Future directions in human-animal bond research. *American Behavioral Scientist*, *47*(1), 79–93. Retrieved from: http://doi.org/10.1177/0002764203255214

Carlsson, C. (2016). A narrative review of qualitative and quantitative research in equine-assisted social work or therapy—Addressing gaps and contradictory results. *Animalia, An Anthrozoology Journal*. Retrieved from: https:// animaliajournal.com/2016/02/14/a-narrative-review-of-qualitative-and-quantitative-research-in-equine- assisted-social-work-or-therapy-addressing-gaps-and-contradictory-results/

Creswell, J.W. (2013). *Research design: Qualitative, quantitative, and mixed methods approaches* (4th edition). Boston, MA: Sage Publications.

Creswell, J.W., & Poth, C.N. (2017). *Qualitative inquiry and research design: Choosing among five approaches* (4th edition). Boston, MA: Sage Publications.

Cuthill, I.C. (2007). Ethical regulation and animal science: Why animal behaviour is not so special. *Animal Behaviour*, *74*(1), 15–22. Retrieved from: http://doi.org/10.1016/j.anbehav.2007.04.002

Esposito, L., Mccune, S., Griffin, J.A., & Maholmes, V. (2011). Directions in human-animal interaction research: Child development, health, and therapeutic interventions. *Child Development Perspectives*, *5*(3), 205–211. Retrieved from: http://doi.org/10.1111/j.1750-8606.2011.00175.x

Hill, C. (2006). *How to think like a horse: The essential handbook for understanding why horses do what they do*. Storey Publishing, LLC.

Hockenhull, J., & Creighton, E. (2012). The strengths of statistical techniques in identifying patterns underlying apparently random behavioral problems in horses. *Journal of Veterinary Behavior: Clinical Applications and Research*, *7*(5), 305–310. Retrieved from: http://doi.org/10.1016/j.jveb.2011.11.001

Huff, D. (1993). *How to lie with statistics*. New York: W. W. Norton & Company.

Leedy, P.D., & Ormrod, J.E. (2015). *Practical research: Planning and design* (11th edition). Pearson.

Martin, P., & Bateson, P. (2007). *Measuring behaviour: An introductory guide* (2nd edition). Cambridge, UK: Cambridge University Press.

Meagher, R.K. (2009). Observer ratings: Validity and value as a tool for animal welfare research. *Applied Animal Behaviour Science*, *119*(1–2), 1–14. Retrieved from: http://doi.org/10.1016/j.applanim.2009.02.026

Phillips Parshall, D. (2003). Research and reflection: Animal assisted therapy in mental health settings. *Counseling and Values*, *48*, 47–56.

Pierard, M., Hall, C., König von Borstel, U., Averis, A., Hawson, L., McLean, A., Nevinson, Visser, K., & McGreevy, P. (2015). Evolving protocols for research in equitation science. *Journal of Veterinary Behavior: Clinical Applications and Research*, *10*(3), 255–266. Retrieved from: http://doi.org/10.1016/j.jveb.2015.01.006

Straus, S.E., Glasziou, P., Richardson, W.S., & Haynes, R.B. (2010). *Evidence-based medicine: How to practice and teach it* (4th edition). London, UK: Churchill Livingstone.

Thodberg, K., Berget, B., & Lidfors, L. (2014). Research in the use of animals as a treatment for humans. *Animal Frontiers*, *4*(3), 43–48. Retrieved from: http://doi.org/10.2527/af.2014-0021

Tuyttens, F.A.M., de Graaf, S., Heerkens, J.L.T., Jacobs, L., Nalon, E., Ott, S., Stadig, L., Van Laer, E., & Ampe, B. (2014). Observer bias in animal behaviour research: Can we believe what we score, if we score what we believe? *Animal Behaviour*, *90*, 273–280. Retrieved from: http://doi.org/10.1016/j.anbehav.2014.02.007

Wathan, J., Burrows, A.M., Waller, B.M., & McComb, K. (2015). EquiFACS: The equine facial action coding system. *PLoS One*, *10*(8), 137818. Retrieved from: http://doi.org/10.1371/journal.pone.0131738

Wilson, C.C., & Barker, S.B. (2003). Challenges in designing human-animal interaction research. *American Behavioral Scientist*, *47*(1), 16–28.

Websites

American Hippotherapy Association Research and Grants www.americanhippotherapyassociation.org/historical-research/

American Occupational Therapy Association Conducting Research www.aota.org/Practice/Researchers/ConductingResearch.aspx

American Physical Therapy Association Section on Research www.ptresearch.org/article/2/about-us

American Psychological Association Responsible Conduct in Research www.apa.org/research/responsible/index.aspx

American Speech-Language-Hearing Association Ethics in Research www.asha.org/Research/Ethics-in-Research/

Association for Assessment and Research in Counseling http://aarc-counseling.org/about-us

Collaborative Institutional Training Initiative (CITI Program) https://about.citiprogram.org/en/homepage/

Horses and Humans Research Foundation www.horsesandhumans.org

5   The Clinical Practice of Equine-Assisted Therapy

☐ Chapter Five Summary

Although equine-assisted therapy takes place in a non-conventional setting, it is not a separate type of therapy, and licensed providers must adhere to the same laws, ethics, standards, and boundaries associated with their conventional healthcare practices.

The non-conventional farm setting can create additional ethical and legal challenges that licensed professionals and the program directors or staff who manage the clinical services must address. In essence, those who oversee the provision of equine-assisted therapy services at a farm are healthcare administrators. This means they must be trained to understand, adapt, and implement healthcare laws, standards, ethics, policies, procedures, and protocols in the equine-assisted therapy setting.

As with any treatment, equine-assisted therapy is not right for every patient all the time. There are precautions and contraindications to consider, and careful assessment and on-going evaluation is necessary to protect the patient. Licensed professionals are expected to act ethically, and use clinical reasoning to determine which patients are right for intervention.

Licensed professionals can choose between a wide variety of models, methods, approaches, and activities when including horses in human healthcare. Understanding the various options and using clinical reasoning to develop a treatment plan that includes horses and the farm milieu is an essential step for professionals interested in providing equine-assisted therapy.

☐ Key Concepts

- Given the lack of conclusive evidence, and the investigational nature of equine-assisted therapy, it is not yet possible to state with any certainty that equine-assisted therapy is clinically indicated for a specific population.
- Equine-assisted therapy presents unique circumstances and additional risk not found in other clinical settings.
- Use of a well-written and comprehensive informed consent document can help patients understand the risks and potential benefits associated with this novel treatment and can help patients make important decisions about participating in equine-assisted therapy.
- Even after careful assessment suggests a patient is appropriate for equine-assisted therapy, there may be times in treatment when the patient will be better served in an office setting.

- There are a variety of different methods licensed mental health professionals can use when providing equine-assisted mental health. It is unlikely that one model or method will fit all patients, and thus licensed mental health professionals are urged to learn multiple approaches to including horses in mental healthcare.
- Facility considerations like upkeep, accessibility, animal care, confidentiality, and the staff and volunteers with whom patients might engage while at the facility are all important factors to take into account when providing equine-assisted therapy.
- Learning to design an equine-assisted therapy session takes training, education, and practice. There are many moving parts to consider that can have a significate impact on treatment outcomes.

☐ Learning Objectives

1. Describe how to assess a patient for equine-assisted therapy, and explain the use of an informed consent document.
2. Identify four models or approaches used when providing equine-assisted therapy.
3. Develop a treatment plan for a patient incorporating horses and the farm milieu.
4. Identify the unique considerations specific to providing regulated healthcare services in a non-conventional setting.

☐ Relevant Terminology

Clinical Reasoning: A process of critical thinking that is informed by education, training, experience, and current research that leads to a reasonable decision about patient care.

Conventional Healthcare: Types of healthcare services that are widely accepted and considered standard or common by most professionals.

HIPAA Standards: A privacy rule that protects confidential patient medical records and information, and allows patients access to their own medical records.

Hippotherapy: Refers to how occupational, physical, and speech therapists incorporate equine movement and the farm milieu in a patient's treatment plan.

Informed Consent: A two-part process in which the healthcare professional provides information based upon scientific research and current practice about a treatment service, approach, strategy, or method, and the patient is supported in making an educated decision as to whether or not to participate in the treatment.

Investigational: As in "investigational nature"—When there is not enough conclusive empirical evidence to fully support a treatment approach, intervention, or strategy, and more research must be conducted.

PATH Intl. Standards Manual: The Professional Association of Therapeutic Horsemanship, International (PATH Intl.) provides a standards manual that is useful for facilities and businesses providing equine-assisted activities or therapies.

Sensory Trail: An interactive trail where patients can guide their horses through a variety of obstacles or have different sensory experiences.

Tack Up: Put equipment onto a horse such as a saddle, bareback pad, or bridle.

☐ Questions to Explore

Use information presented in *The Clinical Practice of Equine-Assisted Therapy: Including Horses in Human Healthcare*, the recommended resources provided in this chapter of the workbook, and your own knowledge and experience to reflect on the following questions.

1. Describe the types of questions you might ask while assessing a patient to determine if equine-assisted therapy is appropriate.

   _____

   _____

   _____

   _____

2. What is the difference between a precaution and a contraindication? How would you address a precaution differently than a contraindication?

   _____

   _____

   _____

   _____

3. What precautions and contraindications should be taken into account when considering if a patient is appropriate for equine-assisted therapy?

   _____

   _____

   _____

   _____

4. What content should be included in an informed consent document for equine-assisted therapy? Also, explain how the results of current research should be represented in an informed consent document.

   _____

   _____

   _____

   _____

5. Why is it still difficult to state with any level of assurance if equine-assisted therapy is indicated for specific populations or conditions? How should this information be presented in an informed consent document?

_____

_____

_____

_____

6. Describe circumstances that could lead you to see a patient in an office setting rather than at the farm interacting with horses.

_____

_____

_____

_____

7. Describe hippotherapy (include the types of professionals who provide it, what training and certification they might have, and common treatment goals) and discuss what patients might be best served through this treatment strategy.

_____

_____

_____

_____

8. Describe equine-facilitated psychotherapy (include the types of professionals who provide it, what training and certification they might have, and common treatment goals) and discuss what patients might be best served through this treatment approach.

_____

_____

_____

_____

9. Describe the EAGALA model of equine-assisted psychotherapy (include the types of professionals who provide it, what training and certification they might have, and common treatment goals) and discuss what patients might be best served through this treatment approach.

_____

_____

_____

_____

10. Describe equine-assisted counseling (include the types of professionals who provide it, what training and certification they might have, and common treatment goals) and discuss what patients might be best served through this treatment approach.

_____

_____

_____

_____

11. List the unique challenges inherent in providing a regulated healthcare service in a non-conventional setting like the farm. Discuss how a provider of equine-assisted therapy should address these issues.

_____

_____

_____

_____

☐ Practical Scenario: Case Study and Treatment Planning

Develop a case study based upon your area of clinical practice (physical, occupational, or speech therapy, or mental health). Include the patient's age, gender, presenting condition(s) and level of functionality, limitations and strengths, physical or mental health history, medications, family/ marital history and/or current relationships, likes or dislikes, lifestyle habits or patterns, and possible precautions or contraindications.

_____

_____

_____

_____

_____

_____

_____

Complete the following treatment plan information based upon your case study, and assuming the patient will be treated using some type of equine-assisted therapy.

1. List the patient's treatment goals.

_____

_____

_____

_____

2. Identify the type of service (physical, occupational, speech, or mental health therapy) that will be used to address those goals.

_____

_____

_____

_____

3. Identify the specific type of equine-assisted therapy that will be utilized. Discuss which method, model, or treatment will be used. Explain your clinical rationale for using this specific type of equine-assisted therapy for this patient.

_____

_____

_____

_____

4. Discuss the context in which equine-assisted therapy will take place. Is it a group session, an individual session, or a family or couples session. How long will each session last, and over what duration of time will treatment take place?

_____

_____

_____

_____

5. Describe the types of activities you might use to address the patient's treatment goals. Explain the clinical reasoning you used to choose these activities. Practice writing a session goal with corresponding activities using clinical language.

_____

_____

_____

_____

6. What animals and human staff or volunteers will participate in the session? Describe why you made the decisions you did in this area.

_____

_____

_____

_____

7. In what location will the session take place? Describe the setting, and discuss safety considerations as well as clinical considerations. Address what equipment you might need during the session.

_____

_____

_____

_____

8. Discuss how you might personally prepare for the session, and how you might help your animals and human staff or volunteers to prepare.

_____

_____

_____

_____

9. Discuss how you will conduct pre/post-clinical evaluations to help determine the effectiveness of the intervention. What types of questions might you include in your evaluation?

_____

_____

_____

_____

☐ Hands-On Activity: Site Visit Part One—Facility Assessment

Description: This is a two-part activity. The second component will take place in Chapter Six. You may choose to combine these two activities into one site visit. It will involve choosing one or more facilities to visit and assess, and interviewing professionals offering equine-assisted therapy. If you have your own facility, it is highly recommended that you use that facility as one of those you assess, but you should also seek out another facility to compare and contrast with your own.

Amount of Time: 2 hours.

Directions: This segment of the activity involves learning how to objectively assess a facility. One of the challenges the industry of equine-assisted therapy faces is that clinical services are provided in settings that may not meet conventional healthcare standards. This can lead to ethical, legal, and in some cases, safety breaches that have the potential to jeopardize the welfare of the patients and the long-term viability of the industry.

Refer to the PATH Intl. standards manual and use this set of questions to evaluate the facility.

1. What is the relationship between the licensed professional and the facility (e.g. is the professional a contractor, do they rent a portion of the facility, do they own the facility, or are they employed at the facility)? Is there a written contract in place that outlines this arrangement?

   _____

   _____

   _____

   _____

2. Does the facility meet licensing, zoning, building, and accessibility codes for the type of services provided?

   _____

   _____

   _____

   _____

3. Does the facility maintain its own equine-assisted therapy liability insurance?

   _____

   _____

   _____

   _____

4. Do each of the professionals who offer equine-assisted therapy services at the facility carry their own malpractice and equine liability insurance?

_____

_____

_____

_____

5. What competency standards are required for professionals to provide equine-assisted therapy services at this facility?

_____

_____

_____

_____

6. Is there a written risk management plan for providing equine-assisted therapy? Are staff, volunteers, and licensed professionals trained to implement this plan?

_____

_____

_____

_____

7. Are there written policies and procedures that include animal care and wellbeing, and administrative, facility, and clinical considerations?

_____

_____

_____

_____

8. How is the facility maintained?

_____ Does it appear well cared for and clean?
_____ Do both indoor and outdoor spaces meet conventional healthcare standards and have:

     _____ Fire extinguishers
     _____ Fire alarms
     _____ Posted emergency and evacuation procedures
     _____ An accessible telephone with clearly posted emergency contact information
     _____ Lighted exit signs
     _____ Sprinklers
     _____ ADA accessibility
     _____ Sanitary bathrooms with hand soap and paper towels (or air dryer)
     _____ Locked medication storage for animal and human medications
     _____ Secure record keeping

9. The following are ways in which a facility can help to address some of the unique concerns associated with providing regulated healthcare in a non-conventional setting. Identify which of these risk mitigation strategies the facility is currently using.

_____ Is the facility fully fenced, with a gated entrance?
_____ Is there signage that guides arriving patients to parking, check in, and waiting areas?
_____ Is there a system in place for checking patients in and monitoring visitors?
_____ Is there a waiting area that is separated visually and acoustically from the treatment spaces?
_____ Is this waiting area clean, professional, welcoming, and monitored?
_____ Are treatment areas separated visually from public areas?
_____ Are treatment areas acoustically private from public areas?
_____ Are public and private (or confidential) areas well marked?
_____ Is there a system for identifying areas where confidential healthcare services are taking place so that other people do not enter?
_____ Is there a private indoor treatment room?
_____ Is there a private area for confidential conversations between staff?
_____ Is the treatment equipment up-to-date, safe, and well maintained?
_____ Are patient records maintained in a way that meets HIPAA standards?
_____ Are staff and volunteers trained to work in a healthcare setting, especially with regard to patient confidentiality, healthcare standards and laws, and professional conduct?

10. Is there enough accessible parking?

_____

_____

_____

_____

11. Do the staff, volunteers, or other professionals you encountered on your visit present themselves in a professional and welcoming manner that is similar to what you might experience in a conventional healthcare setting?

_____

_____

_____

_____

12. How are the animals who live at the facility cared for? Do they appear healthy and fit? Do they have:

_____ Shelter
_____ Clean water
_____ A balanced diet
_____ Appropriate hoof care
_____ Regular veterinary care
_____ Alternative healthcare care options
_____ An exercise and conditioning regime
_____ Hygienic living areas
_____ Ample turn-out space and a daily turn-out schedule
_____ Social interaction opportunities (with each other, not people) and free time away from people

13. Are there opportunities for the patients to engage with other animals or different aspects of nature like a garden or a nature trail?

_____

_____

_____

_____

14. Note which of the following the facility has:

_____ An indoor area
_____ An outdoor area
_____ A round or smaller square pen
_____ A pasture or large turn-out space where patients can observe horses in a more natural setting
_____ A sensory trail
_____ An area to tie, groom, and tack up horses
_____ A waiting room or waiting area
_____ A bathroom

☐ Journal Entry

Use these questions as an opportunity to explore your own ideas, thoughts, feelings, and personal reflections.

1. What was it like evaluating the facility? What did you learn? If you were able to visit multiple facilities, how did these vary based upon the type of services offered?

    _____

    _____

    _____

    _____

2. During your visit, did you feel like you were at a healthcare facility? Why or why not? How might the facility adapt and adjust to meet healthcare standards?

    _____

    _____

    _____

    _____

3. Why is it important an equine-assisted therapy facility adhere to healthcare standards?

    _____

    _____

    _____

    _____

4. After the treatment planning exercise and the hands-on experience of visiting facilities, discuss which patients may be a good fit for equine-assisted therapy, and which might not be. Why or why not? How does the added risk of equine-assisted therapy and the non-conventional setting play into your thinking process?

    _____

    _____

    _____

    _____

☐ **Resources**

Books & Articles

Adams, N., & Grieder, D.M. (2013). *Treatment planning for person-centered care: Shared decision making for whole health* (2nd edition). Cambridge, MA: Academic Press.

American Hippotherapy Association, Inc. (AHA, Inc.). (2017). *Statements of Best Practice for the Use of Hippotherapy by Occupational Therapy, Physical Therapy, and Speech-Language Pathology Professionals*. Retrieved from: www.americanhippotherapyassociation.org/wp-content/uploads/2015/02/Final-2017-Best-Practice.pdf

American Physical Therapy Association (APTA). (2014). *Guide to Physical Therapist Practice 3.0*. Retrieved from: http://guidetoptpractice.apta.org/

American Speech-Language-Hearing Association (ASHA). (2015). *Speech-Language Pathology Medical Review Guidelines*. Retrieved from: www.asha.org/uploadedFiles/SLP-Medical-Review-Guidelines.pdf

Boyd-Franklin, N., & Bry, B.H. (2001). *Reaching out in family therapy: Home-based, school, and community interventions* (1st edition). New York, NY: The Guilford Press.

Burgon, H. (2014). *Equine-assisted therapy and learning with at-risk young people*. London, UK: Palgrave Macmillan.

Buzel, A.H. (2016). *Beyond words: The healing power of horses*. Bloomington, IN: AuthorHouse.

Carr, R.F. (2014). *Health Care Facilities*. Retrieved from: www.wbdg.org/building-types/health-care-facilities

Cook, R. (2013). *Brown Pony Series: Book One: Introduction to hippotherapy*. CreateSpace Independent Publishing Platform.

Cook, R. (2016). *Incorporating games in hippotherapy: Companion book to the Brown Pony Series*. CreateSpace Independent Publishing Platform.

Dunning, A. (2017). *The horse leads the way: Honoring the true role of the horse in equine facilitated practice*. Bishopscastle, UK: YouCaxton Publications.

Engel, B., & MacKinnon, J.R. (2007). *Enhancing human occupation through hippotherapy: A guide for occupational therapy*. Bethesda, MD: AOTA Press.

Hallberg, L. (2008). *Walking the way of the horse: Exploring the power of the horse-human relationship*. Bloomington, IN: iUniverse.

Huber, F., & Wells, C. (2006). *Therapeutic exercise: Treatment planning for progression*. St. Louis, MO: W.B. Saunders.

Kaplan, S.L. (2006). *Outcome measurement and management: First steps for the practicing clinician*. Philadelphia, PA: F.A. Davis Company.

Kirby, M. (2016). *An introduction to equine assisted psychotherapy: Principles, theory, and practice of the Equine Psychotherapy Institute Model*. Bloomington, IN: Balboa Press AU.

Knapp, S. (2013). *More than a mirror: Horses, humans & therapeutic practices*. Marshall, NC: Horse Sense of the Carolinas, Inc.

Lac, V. (2017). *Equine-facilitated psychotherapy and learning: The Human-Equine Relational Development (HERD) Approach*. Cambridge, MA: Academic Press.

Landis, K., Woude, J.V., & Jongsma, A.E. (2004). *The speech-language pathology treatment planner*. Hoboken, NJ: Wiley.

Lincoln, J. (2010). *Exercises for therapeutic riding*. Prescott, AZ: Ralston Store Publishing.

Mandrell, P.J. (2006). *Introduction to equine-assisted psychotherapy*. Maitland, FL: Xulon Press.

McGeeney, A. (2016). *With nature in mind: The ecotherapy manual for mental health professionals*. London, UK: Jessica Kingsley Publishers.

Nussen, J. (2012). *Soul recovery: Equine assisted activities for healing from abuse by others, loss of others & loss of self*. CreateSpace Independent Publishing Platform.

Parent, I.B. (2016a). *The fundamentals of equine assisted trauma therapy: With practical examples from working with members of the armed forces*. CreateSpace Independent Publishing Platform.

Parent, I.B. (2016b). *Teamwork in equine assisted teams*. CreateSpace Independent Publishing Platform.

Perkins, B.L. (2016). *Counseling in nature with at-risk adolescents: Equine assisted psychotherapy and low rope techniques*. CreateSpace Independent Publishing Platform.

Professional Association of Therapeutic Horsemanship, International (PATH Intl.). (2014). *Standards for Certification & Accreditation*. Retrieved from: www.pathintl.org/images/pdf/standards-manual/2014/2014-COMPLETE-PATH-Intl-Standards-Manual.pdf

Rudolph, C. (2015). *The art of facilitation, with 28 equine assisted activities*. Rising Moon Ranch.

Scaffa, M.E., & Reitz, M.S. (2013). *Occupational therapy in community-based practice settings* (2nd edition). Philadelphia, PA: P.A. Davis Company.

Scott, N., & Evans, J.W. (2005). *Special needs, special horses: A guide to the benefits of therapeutic riding*. Denton, TX: University of North Texas Press.

Shambo, L. (2013). *The listening heart: The limbic path beyond office therapy*. Chehalis, WA: Human-Equine Alliances for Learning (HEAL).

Spink, J. (1993). *Development riding therapy*. Communication Skill Builders.

Thomas, L., & Lytle, M. (2016). *Transforming therapy through horses: Case stories teaching the EAGALA model in action*. CreateSpace Independent Publishing Platform.

Trotter, K.S. (2011). *Harnessing the power of equine assisted counseling: Adding animal assisted therapy to your practice*. New York, NY: Routledge.

Websites

American Counseling Association (ACA) Knowledge Center Clearing House www.counseling.org/knowledge-center/clearinghouses

Equine-Assisted Therapy Training and/or Certificate Programs

Adventures in Awareness (AIA) www.adventuresinawareness.net
American Hippotherapy Association, Inc. (AHA) www.americanhippotherapyassociation.org
Eponaquest www.eponaquest.com
Equine Assisted Growth and Learning Association (EAGALA) www.eagala.org
Equine Psychotherapy Institute www.equinepsychotherapy.net.au
Gestalt Equine Institute of the Rockies (GEIR) www.gestaltequineinstitute.com
High Hopes Therapeutic Riding http://highhopestr.org/learn/training-education/
Horse Sense of the Carolinas http://horsesenseotc.com/for-eap-professionals/
Human-Equine Alliances for Learning (HEAL) www.humanequinealliance.com
Human-Equine Relational Development Institute (HERD) www.herdinstitute.com
LEAP Equine www.leapequine.com/
Professional Association of Therapeutic Horsemanship, International (PATH Intl.) www.pathintl.org

6 The Business of Providing Equine-Assisted Therapy

☐ Chapter Six Summary

Little is known about the practice patterns of licensed healthcare professionals offering equine-assisted therapy. Understanding practice patterns includes learning about the demographics of the professionals who provide the service, who they treat, how much they charge, how they bill, what clinical approaches they use, how patients are referred to them, and what business models they use.

The few studies that have been conducted begin to show an emerging pattern that is helpful when conceptualizing the future of the industry and its unique role in human healthcare. However, many more large-scale studies must be conducted to help the industry define, articulate, value, and advocate for the use of equine-assisted therapy.

At present, it appears that mental health professionals represent the largest professional group offering equine-assisted therapy. This is followed by physical therapists, occupational therapists, speech therapists, and last nurses and other medical professionals. Healthcare professionals provide equine-assisted therapy at adaptive riding centers, shared private horse facilities, public horse boarding facilities, or at their own homes.

Most licensed professionals who offer equine-assisted therapy do so on a part-time basis, and many report challenges with financial viability. Most attribute this to the expense of owning and caring for horses, the cost of the facilities needed to provide equine-assisted therapy, and the challenges related to reimbursement for services.

Insurance reimbursement is a complicated topic of discussion and debate within the equine-assisted therapy industry. Since many healthcare providers (and their patients) in the United States rely upon insurance as a way to pay for clinical services, the fact that many insurance companies will not reimburse for equine-assisted therapy is concerning. At present, the majority of insurance companies suggest that equine-assisted therapy is investigational in nature due to the lack of conclusive high-quality research results. Due to this, many patients must pay out of pocket rather than use their insurance. This reduces the number of patients who can afford treatment, and puts pressure on providers and organizations to decrease session fees.

☐ Key Concepts

• Understanding the various business models and choosing the best model for the individual therapist and therapy type is a very important first step in designing a sustainable and financially viable equine-assisted therapy practice.

- There are creative ways to embrace conventional healthcare business models when offering equine-assisted therapy.
- Licensed professionals have a number of options when it comes to deciding upon what facility arrangements to make, including renting the use of space at an existing facility, offering services on a contractual basis, using their own homes, or building a new facility.
- Licensed healthcare professionals must be careful about how they interact with insurance companies and document their services. It is essential that they do not misrepresent what they did with the patient during a session, and thus perpetrate insurance fraud, but they must also use language that insurance companies can understand and relate to.
- Undercharging for equine-assisted therapy devalues the industry, and contributes to the financial instability many professionals experience.
- Many people offer equine-assisted therapy as a "labor of love" because of their own beliefs, experiences, and personal passions. In some cases, providers of equine-assisted therapy may not be skilled at running a business, and this can lead a variety of challenges.
- Including other animals and nature experiences in clinical practice can be a cost savings, and may allow for smaller and more urban facilities which can be more accessible for a greater number of patients.
- Developing a budget, a business plan, a strategic plan, policies, procedures, and forms are important components to running a successful business.

☐ Learning Objectives

1. Identify how understanding professional practice patterns can influence the development of an industry.
2. Identify the different business models professionals might use when providing equine-assisted therapy.
3. Describe the challenges with insurance billing, and identify appropriate language to use.
4. Demonstrate the ability to apply components of a business plan to a practical scenario.
5. Analyze personal levels of business acumen.
6. Identify important components to running a business, and demonstrate the ability to think critically.

☐ Relevant Terminology

Brand: A brand is the business' identity. It shows who the business is and how it operates. The brand is directly connected to the business's mission, vision, and core values. Branding includes the look and feel of the business as manifested in print and digital marketing materials, staff training, customer service, and the way the facility is cared for.

Business Acumen: Business skills or a "business sense" that leads people to be savvy and effective in their business practices.

Contractor: As in "independent contractor"—someone who is not employed by a business and is subject to self-employment tax. An independent contractor is responsible for deciding how to accomplish the task or work, and the person paying the independent contractor can only control the result of the work, not how the task or work is accomplished.

LLC (Limited Liability Corporation): A corporate structure in which the owner or members cannot be held personally liable for the business debts.

Non-Profit: A federal tax designation in which the organization is tax-exempt status from the IRS, and not required to pay state or federal taxes. Although a profit can be made, non-profit organizations are not allowed to distribute this profit in any manner to anyone controlling the organization except through salaries.

PLLC (Professional Liability Corporation): The same as an LLC, except only for licensed professionals.

Private Practice: A business designation in which a professional is the owner of his/her own small business and subject to self-employment taxes.

Sole Proprietor: The simplest type of business structure. It is a non-legal entity in which the owner/operator is personally responsible for the business and all its debts.

Target Market: A group of consumers that a business wishes to serve.

☐ Questions to Explore

Use information presented in *The Clinical Practice of Equine-Assisted Therapy: Including Horses in Human Healthcare*, the recommended resources provided in this chapter of the workbook, and your own knowledge and experience to reflect on the following questions.

1. Why is it important for an industry to conduct professional practice surveys? How might the results of these surveys help professionals?

_____

_____

_____

_____

2. Describe the different business models a professional might choose between when providing equine-assisted therapy. Discuss the pros and cons of each model.

_____

_____

_____

_____

3. Consider the idea that program directors or other staff who manage the provision of equine-assisted therapy services are, in essence, healthcare administrators. How does this shift in thinking change the responsibilities and training necessary for these staff members?

_____

_____

_____

_____

4. Discuss the challenges related to financial viability and accessibly of equine-assisted therapy. How might you address these challenges in your own practice?

_____

_____

_____

_____

5. Describe the potential challenges and benefits associated with offering a clinical service as a passion or "labor of love," include financial and ethical considerations.

_____

_____

_____

_____

6. How could equine-assisted therapy more closely align with conventional healthcare practices and business models?

_____

_____

_____

_____

7. Discuss how you might document the equine-assisted therapy services you provide when corresponding with insurance companies. What language should you avoid, and how can you protect yourself from mistakenly perpetrating insurance fraud?

_____

_____

_____

_____

8. Describe the possible pros and cons of the different facility options a licensed professional has when considering providing equine-assisted therapy.

_____

_____

_____

_____

9. What additional considerations should you take into account if you want to offer equine-assisted therapy out of your own home?

_____

_____

_____

_____

10. What business challenges have you observed in other equine-assisted therapy programs, or what challenges have you personally experienced providing equine-assisted therapy?

_____

_____

_____

_____

☐ **Practical Scenario: Developing a Business Plan**

Use the following questions to develop a business plan. If you have an already existing business, use the information from your business to develop this plan. If you don't have a business, use this activity to conceptualize what type of equine-assisted therapy business you might want.

1. Describe your business. Include its history, your vision for the business, and the business structure or model (private practice sole proprietor, LLC or PLLC, or non-profit).

_____

_____

_____

_____

2. Describe the services provided. Include what populations you will serve and which populations the business is not prepared to serve, and your fee structure.

_____

_____

_____

_____

3. Describe how the business will be administered. Include the location, any relationships with other entities (contracts, grant fulfillment, etc.), the staffing plan, insurance reimbursement, billing, liability insurance, and key aspects of a risk management plan.

_____

_____

_____

_____

4. Discuss your market analysis, including who your target market is, how much people typically pay for services, your competition and what it offers, the strengths and weaknesses of other similar businesses and how those businesses are functioning, and any other observations about market trends.

_____

_____

_____

_____

5. Discuss your marketing plan, including how your business stands out in the marketplace, how you will attract business, how you will alert the community to your presence, and what your brand is.

_____

_____

_____

_____

6. Create a basic pro forma (or projected budget), including income and expenses for running your business.

_____

_____

_____

_____

☐ Business Competency Self-Assessment

As with all other self-assessments in this workbook, this one is meant to help you assess your competency and should be used for personal reflection and to guide the acquisition of knowledge. It is for your eyes only, unless you choose to share the results with a mentor, supervisor or a peer. Try not to be judgmental of your responses and be as honest and authentic as possible. This is meant to be a tool for you to use as you continue to grow and learn as a professional.

Use the following system to rank your level of professional competency—The higher the total score, the more competent you view yourself in that area.

_____ **1**= Beginner or novice (minimal experience, lacking expertise)
_____ **2**= Intermediate (1–5 years of experience, currently developing expertise through specialty education and training)
_____ **3**= Advanced (5+ years of extensive experience with past specialty education and training)
_____ **4**= Expert (10+ years of experience, university-level education, and past specialty education and training)

Leadership Skills

_____ Ability to remain cool, calm, and collected, and inspire confidence
_____ Trustworthiness
_____ Integrity and honesty
_____ Self-direction and self-motivation
_____ Commitment and dedication to the vision and the ability to motivate others
_____ Friend-raising (connecting people to the organization or business)
_____ Ability to clearly explain concepts so that others understand and feel included and part of the team
_____ Delegation and comfortability with others taking the lead
_____ Ability to offer guidance and support for staff
_____ Ability to supervise staff and conduct staff training
_____ Time management
_____ Listening skills
_____ Communication skills
_____ **TOTAL SCORE**

Strategic, Analytic, and Logical Thinking Skills

_____ Hold a clear vision for the business, and effectively communicate that vision with others
_____ Ability to prioritize and effectively execute tasks while meeting deadlines
_____ Strategic planning skills
_____ Ability to gather, evaluate, and present information without personal biases or being overly emotional
_____ Detail oriented and precise
_____ Ability to remain focused on the big picture while understanding and implementing the steps necessary to accomplish strategic goals
_____ **TOTAL SCORE**

©2018, *The Equine-Assisted Therapy Workbook: A Learning Guide for Professionals and Students*, Leif Hallberg, Routledge

Financial Acumen

_____ Budget preparation skills

_____ Ability to understand spreadsheets and financial statements

_____ Ability to understand financial reports

_____ Formal accounting skills or the ability to develop an accounting system

_____ Use of financial performance metrics

_____ Ability to develop financial strategies and effectively communicate and implement those strategies

_____ Ability to develop a fee scale

_____ Ability to develop and manage a billing and collections system

_____ Fundraising (non-profit only)

_____ Grant writing (non-profit only)

_____ **TOTAL SCORE**

Marketing Skills

_____ Creativity and innovation

_____ Developing a brand platform and business identity

_____ Ability to conduct or oversee a market analysis and know how to use the results effectively

_____ Understanding of social media and other digital marketing techniques

_____ Understanding of public relations strategies

_____ Technological skills

_____ Verbal and non-verbal communication skills especially related to explaining the business and the business's services to others

_____ Business negotiations

_____ **TOTAL SCORE**

Other Business Skills

_____ Establishing a business model

_____ Establishing a legal structure

_____ Crafting a business plan

_____ Designing and implementing policies, procedures, and protocols

_____ Designing forms

_____ Understanding HIPAA compliance and maintaining compliant record keeping practice

_____ **TOTAL SCORE**

_____ **TOTAL SELF-ASSESSMENT SCORE**

☐ Hands-On Activity: Site Visit Part Two—Business Practices

Description: This is the second component of the site visit activity. In this segment, you will be asked to interview professionals about their business practices. It is all too common in the equine-assisted therapy industry for licensed professionals to be passionate about their work with horses, but lack solid business practices that ensure long-term stability and enable that the business is financially viable. This activity is designed to help readers think critically about important aspects of setting up and running a business.

Amount of Time: 1 hour.

Directions: This activity can either be done in person while at the facility, or after your visit over the phone or via email.

Business Practices Questions

1. What type of professional license does the professional hold? What services do they provide?

    _____

    _____

    _____

    _____

2. What business model does the professional utilize?

    _____

    _____

    _____

    _____

3. Is there a business plan in place? A strategic plan? A marketing plan? A budget? Ask if you might have a copy of any of these materials.

    _____

    _____

    _____

    _____

4. Is there an organizational chart in place to help people understand hierarchy and communication flow?

_____

_____

_____

_____

5. How does communication and leadership work within the business?

_____ Are there regular meetings to share important updates and information?
_____ Are there systems of written communication to document important information and alert others to that information?
_____ Are there regular staff trainings?
_____ Do the staff and volunteers seem to be on the same page?
_____ Does everyone seem to know what is happening and appear as though they are working together toward the same goals?

6. Does the professional bill insurance for equine-assisted therapy? If so, discuss the language the professional uses, the challenges he/she has faced, and ask for advice in how you might set up a successful insurance billing practice.

_____

_____

_____

_____

7. How is billing conducted? Does the professional do billing themselves, do they outsource, or does that facility provide this service?

_____

_____

_____

_____

8. How much do services cost? Is there a sliding scale? How often does the professional receive 100% payment rather than partial payment (e.g. services cost $140 for a 45-minute hippotherapy session; on average the professional collects $60 per session).

_____

_____

_____

_____

9. Ask for a blank copy of all the forms the professional uses. This is an invaluable resource in developing your own forms, or evaluating your existing forms.

_____

_____

_____

_____

10. What are the biggest business-related challenges the professional faces?

_____

_____

_____

_____

☐ Journal Entry

Use these questions as an opportunity to explore your own ideas, thoughts, feelings, and personal reflections.

1. What did you learn about the business of providing equine-assisted therapy?

_____

_____

_____

_____

2. In your personal experience, what are the biggest challenges you face when considering developing an equine-assisted therapy business or running your existing business?

_____

_____

_____

_____

3. What did you learn from the results of your Business Skills Self-Assessment? How will this knowledge be helpful to you?

_____

_____

_____

_____

4. What remaining questions do you have about running an equine-assisted therapy business, and how might you seek out the answers to those questions?

_____

_____

_____

_____

☐ Resources

Books & Articles

Adams, T. (2005). Founder transitions: Creating good endings and new beginnings. *Executive Transitions*. Retrieved from: www.aecf.org/m/resourcedoc/AECF-FounderTransitions-2005-Full.pdf

American Hippotherapy Association, Inc. (AHA, Inc.). (2016). *AHA, Inc.'s Position on Coding and Billing*. Retrieved from: www.americanhippotherapyassociation.org/wp-content/uploads/2015/02/Approved_Position-On-Coding-and-Billing_Updated-Feb-11_2016.pdf

American Occupational Therapy Association (AOTA). (2017). *Coding and Billing*. Retrieved from: www.aota.org/Advocacy-Policy/Federal-Reg-Affairs/Coding.aspx

American Physical Therapy Association (APTA). (2017). *Coding and Billing*. Retrieved from: www.apta.org/Payment/CodingBilling/

American Speech-Language-Hearing Association (ASHA). (2004). *Preferred Practice Patterns for the Profession of Speech-Language Pathology*. Retrieved from: www.asha.org/policy/PP2004-00191/

American Speech-Language-Hearing Association (ASHA). (2017a). *Interprofessional Practice Survey Results*. Retrieved from: www.asha.org/uploadedFiles/2017-Interprofessional-Practice-Survey-Results.pdf

American Speech-Language-Hearing Association (ASHA). (2017b). *Billing and Reimbursement*. Retrieved from: www.asha.org/practice/reimbursement/

Casady, R. (2012). Insurance task force report. *Hippotherapy: The Official Publication of the American Hippotherapy Association*, Summer, 6–8.

Cook, R. (2014). *Brown Pony Series: Book Four: The business of hippotherapy*. CreateSpace Independent Publishing Platform.

Cook, R. (2015). *Brown Pony Series: Book Three: Considering hippotherapy in your career plans*. CreateSpace Independent Publishing Platform.

Cope, K. (2012). *Seeing the big picture: Business acumen to build your credibility, career, and company*. Austin, TX: Greenleaf Book Group Press.

Grodzki, L. (2015). *Building your ideal private practice: A guide for therapists and other healing professionals* (2nd edition). New York, NY: W. W. Norton & Company.

Hill, C. (2005). *Horsekeeping on a small acreage: Designing and managing your equine facilities* (2nd edition). North Adams, MA: Storey Publishing, LLC.

Knapp, S. (2007). *Horse sense, business sense*. Marshall, NC: Horse Sense of the Carolinas, Inc.

Non-Profit Finance Fund. (2016). *Nonprofit Finance 101*. Retrieved from: www.nonprofitfinancefund.org/nonprofit-finance-101

Renz, D. (2010). *The Jossey-Bass handbook of nonprofit leadership and management* (3rd edition). San Francisco, CA: Jossey-Bass.

Safian, S.C. (2013). *Fundamentals of health care administration*. New York: Pearson.

Shelton, H. (2017). *The secrets to writing a successful business plan: A pro shares a step-by-step guide to creating a plan that gets results*. Rockville, MD: Summit Valley Press.

Teitelbaum, J.B., & Wilensky, S.E. (2012). *Essentials of health policy and law* (2nd edition). Burlington, MA: Jones & Bartlett Learning.

Zietlow, J., Hankin, J.A., & Seidner, A.G. (2007). *Financial management for nonprofit organizations: Policies and practices* (1st edition). Hoboken, NJ: Wiley Publishing.

Websites

American Hippotherapy Association www.americanhippotherapyassociation.org

American Society of Association Executives www.asaecenter.org

Annie A. Casey Foundation www.aecf.org/

Equisure, Inc. www.equisure-inc.com/products/horse-products/

Health Care Administrators Association www.hcaa.org/

Horse Sense of the Carolinas, Inc. www.horsesenseotc.com

Markel Insurance www.markelinsurance.com/horseandfarm
Non-Profit Finance Fund www.nonprofitfinancefund.org
Non-Profit Leadership Alliance www.nonprofitleadershipalliance.org
PATH Intl. www.pathintl.org
Small Business Administration www.sba.gov

7   The Ethics of Appropriating Horses for Human Wellbeing

☐ **Chapter Seven Summary**

When humans appropriate any species of animal for human wellbeing, it is the responsibility of the human to provide the best possible care for that animal. Asking an animal to work in a human healthcare profession is much like asking a human to do the same. Just like humans, animals need time off, exercise, social interactions, and good healthcare, and they need space and distance from their patients and their handlers. Taking into consideration the ethological characteristics of the species can help to guide and direct ethical care protocols.

In some cases, providers of equine-assisted therapy (and probably other forms of animal-assisted therapy) make assumptions that the animal is "happy" or enjoys doing the work based upon their own projections, biases, beliefs, and needs. Meanwhile, it is quite common to visit a facility and observe animals who show obvious signs of stress, pain, or illness, and to hear the caretakers rationalize the animal's condition, or suggest this is how the animal is all the time.

A solid body of research suggests that humans may have a difficult time recognizing the signs of pain, stress, or discomfort in both other humans and animals if they are overexposed to these symptoms. For example, nurses in a hospital setting may become accustomed to seeing people in pain, and thus this state of being becomes normal or expected. Similarly, horse owners or care-takers may become used to the behaviors of horses who are ill, in pain, stressed, or burned out, assuming their behaviors are typical and therefore acceptable. Although objective assessment is likely the best way to address this problem, some horse owners may feel uncomfortable and even threatened by outside evaluation. Also, horse owners are notorious for being highly opinionated, and may be less inclined to accept new ideas or information.

The small amount of research that has been conducted on the effects of equine-assisted therapy on the horses themselves shows that equine-assisted therapy does impact horses. But, exactly how it impacts them or the extent to which it may cause long-term harm is still unknown. Specific activities, populations, and ways of viewing or engaging with horses appear to have more of a negative effect than others. Due to this, it is important for equine-assisted therapy providers to understand how horses demonstrate stress, anxiety, fear, depression, pain, discomfort, and burn-out, and learn to shape human-equine interactions in a way that supports the needs of the horses and reduces negative effects.

The scientific study of horses has not received a great deal of attention until more recently. Common knowledge of horse behavior, physiology, and psychology is typically limited to personal experiences and the wisdom of horse trainers, and usually focuses on opinion-based materials rather than scientific research and academic education in equitation science, equine behavior science, and equine ethology.

Ethically, and from a safety standpoint, providers of equine-assisted therapy have an important responsibly to learn more about horses from a scientific and academic perspective, and invest in more objective and less biased equine assessment and care practices.

☐ Key Concepts

- Equines communicate using a highly developed and relatively clear language that humans can learn to understand. Unfortunately, without education and training, humans commonly misunderstand equine communication and make inaccurate assumptions about equine behavior.
- The idea that the human version of dominance or "leadership" is transferable to horse behavior is inaccurate, and has led to training techniques in which humans unknowingly rely upon fear and confusion to manipulate the horse into submission.
- The signs and signals of fear, distress, confusion, or pain in horses are also commonly misunderstood by humans, resulting in humans using training techniques that trigger an appeasing response from the horse. Humans are likely to assume this response is positive, and may not understand the negative effects of the training technique.
- Learning how to objectively (as much as possible) assess horses is an essential component to providing equine-assisted therapy.
- Horses have many ethological needs that must be attended to for their physical and psychological wellbeing.

☐ Learning Objectives

1. Identify common forms of equine communication and behavior.
2. Differentiate between submissive/appeasing behaviors and engaged curiosity and learning.
3. Identify important ethological needs and how to attend to those needs.
4. Evaluate and analyze your own biases and beliefs about horses.
5. Demonstrate understanding and practical application of objective equine assessment.

☐ Relevant Terminology

Appease: To pacify or placate. Especially in response to an aggressor, often to protect one's self or to remain safe. Usually the behavior is different than what would occur in a healthier or safer situation.

Body Condition Score: A numerical scale used to evaluate the amount of fat on a horse's body. This scale was originally developed by Don Henneke, PhD, and is a standardized scoring system for evaluating equine body condition.

Ethology: The scientific and objective study of animal behavior, especially under natural conditions.

Objective: Impartial or unbiased, not left to personal interpretation.

□ **Questions to Explore**

Use information presented in *The Clinical Practice of Equine-Assisted Therapy: Including Horses in Human Healthcare*, the recommended resources provided in this chapter of the workbook, and your own knowledge and experience to reflect on the following questions.

1. How do you assess for fear, anxiety, stress, burnout or happiness in horses? What objective measures can you use to determine what your horse is experiencing?

_____

_____

_____

_____

2. Describe behaviors commonly associated with submissive or appeasing behaviors. What training techniques or activities may cause a horse to appease or submit? Discuss the difference between a horse who appeases/submits and one who is curious and actively engaged in learning.

_____

_____

_____

_____

3. What activities used in equine-assisted therapy could trigger a fear, confusion, or appeasing response? Why is it important to design activities that diminish this response in horses? How might you adjust the activity so that the horse could have a different, healthier reaction?

_____

_____

_____

_____

4. How can fear, anxiety or confusion in horses impact patients?

_____

_____

_____

_____

5. What are your horse's ethological needs? What systems do you have in place, to attend to those needs and what systems would you like to implement or add?

_____

_____

_____

_____

6. Why is space to roam freely, exercise, proper conditioning, and different types of experiences and activities so important to consider when thinking of the welfare of equine-assisted therapy horses?

_____

_____

_____

_____

7. How does improper riding position impact horse health? Do you think it is ethical to use the horse's movement or riding as a therapeutic tool if a patient is so unbalanced they are causing the horse harm?

_____

_____

_____

_____

8. Do you have a system for objective equine assessment? If so, how does it work? If not, what system might you be able to implement moving forward? What role might outside evaluation play in this system?

_____

_____

_____

_____

9. Do you feel your own equine skills are advanced enough to be able to ethically attend to the needs of the horse(s) and keep your patients safe? If not, what areas would you like to enhance or improve upon?

_____

_____

_____

_____

☐ Practical Scenarios

Read the Scenarios and Answer the Following Questions.

A horse is standing in a pasture. The sun is shining and it is comfortably warm outside. The horse has his back hoof cocked, his tail is swishing quietly, and his ears are drooped off to the sides.

1. What does this body language indicate?

   _____

   _____

   _____

   _____

2. What should you do before approaching this horse?

   _____

   _____

   _____

   _____

A horse suddenly looks up, perks her ears forward, and flares her nostrils.

1. What does this body language indicate?

   _____

   _____

   _____

   _____

2. What should you do (or prepare your patient to do) when a horse behaves in this way?

   _____

   _____

   _____

   _____

A patient begins to approach a horse who is tied. The horse immediately pins his ears and shifts his weight, cocking his back hoof. As the patient continues to advance, the horse begins to swish his tail.

1. What does this body language indicate?

   _____

   _____

   _____

   _____

2. What should you tell your patient to do?

   _____

   _____

   _____

   _____

There are five horses turned out together in a loose herd environment. One of the horses is obviously pushing the others around, causing them to move and shift positions around the pasture. Another horse remains at some distance from the group, attempting to stay away from the ruckus, but when the more "dominant" horse comes near, relinquishes grazing territory to avoid conflict. Over time the "less dominant" horse begins to move back towards the barn, and you notice the herd (including the "dominant" horse) slowly follows.

1. In this scenario, which horse is higher in the herd hierarchy? How can you tell?

   _____

   _____

   _____

   _____

2. How does this scenario highlight the human misunderstanding of pressure, dominance, and leadership, and what can humans learn from horses about leadership?

_____

_____

_____

_____

Six horses are loose in an arena. A group of 20 people enter the arena, form and line with interlocking arms, and attempt to corner each horse individually using a variety of techniques including coaxing, yelling, boxing the horse in, or creating a barrier so the horse cannot return to the rest of the herd.

1. Why might this activity initiate the flight, fight, freeze, appease response?

_____

_____

_____

_____

2. What negative effects could this have on the horse, and would you use this activity clinically? Why or why not?

_____

_____

_____

_____

A horse is loose in a round pen. The patient is told to go into the pen and ask the horse to move. The patient is taught that he will earn the horse's respect if he can get the horse's feet to move, and that this behavior models how horses establish leadership in a natural setting. The patient pushes the horse using his body language and his voice until the horse turns towards him, drops her head, and licks and chews. The professional suggests this behavior shows the horse is connecting with the patient and showing her respect.

1. How does this scenario demonstrate our misunderstanding of equine communication and behavior?

_____

_____

_____

_____

2. What else might make a horse turn in and lick and chew in this scenario, and what might this behavior actually communicate?

_____

_____

_____

_____

3. What does current research tell us about licking and chewing?

_____

_____

_____

_____

4. How might the shape of the pen influence the horse's submissive behaviors?

_____

_____

_____

_____

☐ Hands-On Activity: Equine Assessment

Description: Assessment is essential to better understanding equine welfare. Without an objective tool, it is difficult—if not impossible—to separate out opinions or personal beliefs from facts. This tool supports readers in practicing objective assessment.

Directions: Choose one horse you can assess multiple times in one week. Use the following chart to evaluate the same horse each time. This will give you a fairly good baseline condition for this horse. Ask a colleague to evaluate the same horse at the same time using the same chart. Do not compare results until the end of the week.

Use the "comments" sections to provide further objective detail. For example, document how many gallons of water the horse drank, or how many gut sounds you heard per minute, which leg was injured or sore, or any other detail that would help you objectively evaluate your horse's condition.

This chart should be used regularly to track changes in health and wellbeing, and provide a means to better assess changes in your horse and communicate more clearly with your veterinarian.

Amount of Time: 20–30 minutes at least three times in one week.

Date: _____

Name of Horse: _____ **Age:** _____ **Sex:** _____ **Color:** _____ **Breed:** _____

Attitude and Demeanor: ☐ Bright, Alert, Responsive ☐ Lethargic/Tired ☐ Depressed ☐ Anxious ☐ Unresponsive/Withdrawn

Body Condition Score (1–9): _____

Comments:

Temperature: _____ **Pulse:** _____ **Respiration:** _____ **Capillary Refill Time:** _____

Pulse Feels: ☐ Normal ☐ Weak ☐ Irregular

Heart Sounds: ☐ Normal ☐ Weak ☐ Irregular

Respiratory Sounds: ☐ Normal ☐ Abnormal

Gut Sounds: ☐ Normal ☐ Abnormal

Comments:

Mane/Tail Condition: ☐ Normal ☐ Abnormal ☐ Rough ☐ Dull ☐ Smooth

Skin/Coat Condition: ☐ Normal ☐ Abnormal ☐ Rough ☐ Dull ☐ Smooth

Eyes: ☐ Bright ☐ Dull ☐ Irritated ☐ Runny ☐ Cloudy ☐ Red ☐ Wrinkles around the eye

Head and Body: ☐ Normal ☐ Abnormal ☐ Heat ☐ Swelling ☐ Wounds or injuries

Sheath/Udder: ☐ Normal ☐ Abnormal ☐ Heat ☐ Swelling

Comments:

Drinking: ☐ Normal ☐ Less than normal ☐ More than normal ☐ Not drinking

Eating: ☐ Normal ☐ Less than normal ☐ More than normal ☐ Not eating

Urinating: ☐ Normal ☐ Less than normal ☐ More than normal ☐ Not urinating

Defecating: ☐ Normal ☐ Less than normal ☐ Differently than normal ☐ Not defecating

Comments:

Movement: ☐ Normal ☐ Lame ☐ Sore/Tender ☐ Weak/Wobbly ☐ Not moving

Weight Bearing: ☐ Normal ☐ Uncomfortable ☐ Shifting weight

Limbs Appear: ☐ Normal ☐ Abnormal ☐ Heat ☐ Swelling

Feet Appear: ☐ Normal ☐ Abnormal ☐ Heat ☐ Abnormal pulse

Back Appears: ☐ Normal ☐ Flinching away from pressure ☐ Heat ☐ Swelling

Comments:

Laying Down: ☐ Normal ☐ Less than normal ☐ Differently than normal ☐ Not laying down

Getting Up: ☐ Normal ☐ Harder than normal ☐ Not getting up without help

Socializing: ☐ Normal ☐ Less than normal ☐ Differently than normal ☐ Not socializing

Behavior: ☐ Normal ☐ More aggressive ☐ More passive ☐ Less alert ☐ Less engaged ☐ Isolating ☐ Displaying stereotypical behaviors

Comments:

Overall Health Score: ☐ Excellent ☐ Good ☐ Fair ☐ Poor

Recommendations:

☐ Journal Entry

Use these questions as an opportunity to explore your own ideas, thoughts, feelings, and personal reflections.

1. What did you learn from the equine assessment activity? How comparable were the results between you and your colleague?

    _____

    _____

    _____

    _____

2. What new information did you learn about horses through reading Chapter Seven or exploring the additional resources?

    _____

    _____

    _____

    _____

3. How might this new information inform your equine-assisted therapy practice?

    _____

    _____

    _____

    _____

4. Consider how strong your desire is for horses to "like" equine-assisted therapy. What would you do if you learned equine-assisted therapy was negatively affecting your horses, either physically or mentally?

    _____

    _____

    _____

    _____

☐ **Resources**

Books & Articles

American Society for the Prevention of Cruelty to Animals (ASPCA). (2016). *Five Freedoms.* Retrieved from: http://aspcapro.org/resource/shelter-health-animal-care/five-freedoms

Budiansky, S. (1997). *The nature of horses: Exploring equine evolution, intelligence, and behavior.* New York, NY: The Free Press.

Hamilton, A.J. (2011). *Zen mind, Zen horse: The science and spirituality of working with horses.* North Adams, MA: Storey Publishing, LLC.

Hill, C. (1997). *Horse health care: A step-by-step photographic guide to mastering over 100 horsekeeping skills.* North Adams, MA: Storey Publishing, LLC.

Hill, C. (2006). *How to think like a horse: Essential insights for understanding equine behavior and building an effective partnership with your horse.* North Adams, MA: Storey Publishing, LLC.

Kentucky Equine Research. (2017). *Horse Body Condition Score Chart.* Retrieved from: https://ker.com/tools/library/horse-body-condition-score-chart/

Kiley-Worthington, M. (1997). *Equine welfare.* Ramsbury, UK: J.A. Allen.

McDonnell, S. (2003). *The equid ethogram: A practical field guide to horse behavior.* Lexington, KY: Eclipse Press.

McDonnell, S. (2005). *Understanding your horse's behavior.* Lexington, KY: Eclipse Press.

McDonnell, S. (October 5, 2016). *The Science behind 'Licking and Chewing' in Horses.* Retrieved from: www.thehorse.com/articles/38258/the-science-behind-licking-and-chewing-in-horses

McGreevy, P. (2012). *Equine behavior: A guide for veterinarians and equine scientists* (2nd edition). Philadelphia, PA: Saunders Ltd.

McGreevy, P., & McLean, A. (2010). *Equitation science.* Hoboken, NJ: Wiley-Blackwell.

Mills, D.S., & McDonnell, S.M. (2005). *The domestic horse: The origins, development and management of its behavior.* Cambridge: Cambridge University Press.

Schoen, A., & Gordon, S. (2015). *The compassionate equestrian: 25 principles to live by when caring for and working with horses.* North Pomfret, VT: Trafalgar Square Books.

Waring, G.H. (2007). *Horse behavior* (2nd edition). Norwich, NY: William Andrew.

Websites

American Association of Equine Practitioners https://aaep.org/
American Society for the Prevention of Cruelty to Animals www.aspca.org/
American Veterinary Medical Association www.avma.org
Animal Behavior Society www.animalbehaviorsociety.org/
Animal Health Foundation www.animalhealthfoundation.net/
Kentucky Equine Research https://ker.com/
United States Pony Club www.ponyclub.org

Video

Steward, L. (April 5, 2017). *What Is Your Pet Telling You?* Retrieved from: www.youtube.com/watch?v=oTVlCnenYeE

8 A Vision for the Future

☐ Chapter Eight Summary

There is still so much to be learned about equine-assisted therapy, and the industry is ripe with opportunities to help professionalize the practice. Every professional interested in equine-assisted therapy or already providing equine-assisted therapy has an important role to play. All professionals must work together to build a stronger and more viable foundation, and move the industry forward with greater clarity, definition, and collaboration.

For so many, equine-assisted therapy is provided as a personal passion or labor of love. Horse people are notoriously opinionated and known to disagree with each other frequently. As an industry, professionals must find a way to transcend this tendency, and instead look for ways to agree, collaborate, and support each other. There are many aspects of equine-assisted therapy that aren't really understood, and everyone involved must be open to learning.

The industry has a long way to go before anyone can say with certainty how equine-assisted therapy works, or who it helps. There are hard questions to answer about the effects of equine-assisted therapy on horses, and as new information is gained, professionals may face ethical challenges related to the role of the horse in human healthcare. At one point or other, anyone involved in this industry may have to accept that a long-held belief is not accurate, or is no longer serving the industry, the patients, or the horses, and may have to change or adjust practices. This can be hard, both personally and professionally. But, in order to preserve this industry and advance the clinical practice in a safe and ethical manner, change and growth is inevitable.

☐ Key Concepts

- The various membership associations and training organizations use different terms and definitions, which creates industry-wide confusion and affects both practice and research.
- The lines between therapy and non-therapy services have become blurred in the equine-assisted activities and therapies industry as a whole. Non-licensed professionals frequently offer services that cross into the scope of practice of licensed professionals. This is unethical, and even illegal in some cases.
- There is a general lack of consistency in the competency levels of licensed professionals who provide equine-assisted therapy. The industry has yet to come together to agree upon acceptable competency standards or assessments protocols.
- Until more rigorous research has been conducted that addresses the existing methodological challenges, licensed professionals are urged to accept the investigational nature of equine-assisted therapy.

- Overall, research design must be improved so that results can be compared across multiple studies that use the same protocols. Without this, benefits claims are hard to validate as each study is essentially a stand-alone example and results cannot be generalized.
- Research agendas must be established that include the need for more high-quality research that examines how equine-assisted therapy actually works, the practice patterns of those providing the services, what the effects of equine-assisted therapy are on horses, and even how equine-assisted therapy could prove ineffective for specific populations or conditions.
- Through collaborative efforts, these obstacles can be addressed, and the industry will be better prepared to flourish and grow during the coming years.

☐ Learning Objectives

1. Summarize the challenges facing the equine-assisted therapy industry.
2. Identify ways to personally contribute to the safe and ethical growth and development of the equine-assisted therapy industry.
3. Assess your overall knowledge and understanding of the content provided in both the book and the workbook.

☐ Relevant Terminology

Evidence-Based Practice: Evidence-based practice refers to models, methods, or treatment strategies that integrate the results of high-quality research with clinical expertise, and take into consideration the patient's individual needs, beliefs, and values.

Gallop: The fastest pace for a horse.

Scope of Practice: The procedures, actions, and processes a healthcare professional is allowed to engage in under their licensure, and within state and federal law.

☐ Questions to Explore

Use information presented in *The Clinical Practice of Equine-Assisted Therapy: Including Horses in Human Healthcare*, the recommended resources provided in this chapter of the workbook, and your own knowledge and experience to reflect on the following questions.

1. What do you understand to be the biggest challenges and opportunities for the industry of equine-assisted therapy?

   _____

   _____

   _____

   _____

2. Why is it important to clarify terminology and definitions? What are the challenges in this area? How could you help with this issue?

   _____

   _____

   _____

   _____

3. Describe how non-therapy services may infringe upon the scope of practice of licensed professionals providing equine-assisted therapy. Why is this an important issue? How could you help with this issue?

   _____

   _____

   _____

   _____

4. Why are competency standards important for equine-assisted therapy? How might a lack of competency standards affect patient care? What steps can you take to improve your own competency in equine-assisted therapy?

   _____

   _____

   _____

   _____

5. How do professional fields come together and make big decisions? How might the industry of equine-assisted therapy learn from these examples, and what action steps could the industry take? Is there anything you could do to help?

_____

_____

_____

_____

6. Why is equine-assisted therapy still considered investigational in nature? How might you view this as a positive rather than a negative? What is the potential caution of moving equine-assisted therapy too quickly towards an "evidence-based" practice? What might be missed in this process?

_____

_____

_____

_____

7. What types of research do you think are important to consider when developing a research agenda for equine-assisted therapy?

_____

_____

_____

_____

8. What ethical considerations should equine-assisted therapy providers take into account when appropriating horses for human wellbeing? How might these concerns be addressed?

_____

_____

_____

_____

9. Knowing the challenges the industry faces, how can you be a part of preserving its future?

_____

_____

_____

_____

☐ Biases and Beliefs Self-Assessment

Taking this self-assessment three times throughout the workbook will help you to assess your own level of personal bias. As a reminder, do not go back and read your responses to the first or second self-assessment until you have completed this final assessment. Try to be as honest and authentic as possible. Remember, this is meant for your eyes only, although you may choose to use some of your responses in supervision, or discuss with peers as you feel comfortable. Try not to be judgmental of your responses, rather view this an opportunity to discover something new about yourself. A higher score indicates greater levels of acceptance, open-mindedness, and collaboration.

Rank the following statements accordingly: 1=Strongly disagree, 2 = Disagree, 3 = Unsure or somewhere in the middle, 4 = Agree, 5 = Strongly agree. Total your score at the bottom of the self-assessment. A higher score indicates greater levels of acceptance, open-mindedness, and collaboration.

_____ I am open minded and curious about how other people practice equine-assisted therapy.

_____ I research my beliefs, taking into consideration many different perspectives, and am comfortable changing my opinions based upon what I learn.

_____ I continually strive to learn more about equine-assisted therapy.

_____ I learn from other people's perspectives, and implement their ideas if applicable.

_____ I ask lots of questions and attempt to understand why other people think or believe the way they do.

_____ I see value in everyone's perspectives, and encourage open discussion about differences.

_____ I find collaboration refreshing, helpful, productive, and enjoyable.

_____ I enjoy and seek out collaborative environments or opportunities.

_____ I seek outside/expert support and guidance when making hard clinical decisions.

_____ I believe there are many different ways to work with horses, and I am open to trying new ideas.

_____ I seek outside/expert support and guidance when evaluating my horses' health and wellbeing.

_____ I take the advice of other people when it comes to addressing health and wellness issues with my horses.

_____ I make time to provide help and guidance to those new to the industry, and answer their questions with respect, patience, and open-mindedness.

_____ I welcome newcomers to the industry, and believe they have something to teach me.

_____ I am comfortable referring my patients to other professionals.

_____ When people ask me questions about equine-assisted therapy, I learn from their questions and find myself expanding my own knowledge because of their query.

_____ I make time to learn something new about equine-assisted therapy on a regular basis.

_____ I am easy to approach, and encourage conversation.

_____ I am less likely to judge people, and more likely to learn about them and their beliefs.

_____ I enjoy differences in beliefs and find those differences valuable.

_____ I commonly use peer or professional supervision as a way to check my own decisions and beliefs.

_____ I use scholarly resources such as text books or peer-reviewed journals to inform my opinions and guide my decision making.

_____ I ask the opinions of others and listen to their advice, implementing applicable information.

_____ I am not defensive about my clinical decisions and an open to critique and suggestions.

_____ I am not defensive about my horse care decisions and an open to critique and suggestions.

_____ I don't assume that equine-assisted therapy is right for every patient.

_____ I keep my personal beliefs about how horses might impact people out of the therapy process.

_____ I don't use equine-assisted therapy for every patient, and rather make careful choices about which patients would be best served by the treatment.

_____ I understand and value the investigative nature of equine-assisted therapy.

_____ I don't try to defend equine-assisted therapy as a "proven" clinical intervention, and if research results show less than positive effects, I am open and curious.

_____ I am able to separate my own love for horses from the clinical use of equine-assisted therapy.

_____ I provide equine-assisted therapy first because of the clinical benefits it offers the patient, and second because I enjoy it.

_____ I am open to the idea that working with another animal could produce similar health benefits as working with horses.

_____ I don't need my "way" of working with horses or providing equine-assisted therapy to be "right." I am open to many different approaches.

_____ I model collaborative values, believing this is important to teach patients as well as foster in other professionals.

_____ **TOTAL SCORE**

©2018, _The Equine-Assisted Therapy Workbook: A Learning Guide for Professionals and Students_, Leif Hallberg, Routledge

☐ **Final Exam**

Use this exam as a way to evaluate your own learning. Answers to all of these questions can be found in either this workbook, *The Clinical Practice of Equine-Assisted Therapy: Including Horses in Human Healthcare*, or in one of the resources provided.

1. The scientific and objective study of animal behavior especially under natural conditions is called:

    a. Animal husbandry
    b. Ethology
    c. Anthrozoology

2. Therapy is (circle all that apply):

    a. Regulated by healthcare laws
    b. Provided by anyone
    c. Provided only by licensed (or regulated) healthcare professionals
    d. Used to treat physical or mental illnesses, disorders or diseases
    e. Focused on teaching skills

3. A broad term used to describe both therapy and non-therapy equine-assisted services.

    a. Equine-assisted mental health
    b. Equine-assisted physical therapy
    c. Equine-assisted activities and therapies
    d. Equine-assisted learning

4. When a horse perks one ear forward and one ear back, it indicates the horse is:

    a. Upset or needs space
    b. Excited or attentive
    c. Listening
    d. Sleepy

5. List three different business models that could be used when offering equine-assisted therapy.

    a. _____

    b. _____

    c. _____

6. Equine-assisted therapy is one type of animal-assisted therapy and shares foundational theories related to human-animal bonding.

    a. True
    b. False

7. When a horse is confused, cornered, or cannot escape from pressure, he/she could respond by:

    a. Appeasing
    b. Licking and chewing

c. Submitting
d. "Joining up"
e. All of the above

8. The movement of the horse can be an important treatment tool if appropriately used by a trained physical, occupational, or speech therapist.

   a. True
   b. False

9. The procedures, processes, and actions that a healthcare provider is permitted to undertake by law in keeping with the terms of their professional license is called:

   a. Specialty area of practice
   b. Treatment intervention
   c. Scope of practice
   d. Treatment strategy

10. List five components that should be included in a business plan.

    a. _____

    b. _____

    c. _____

    d. _____

    e. _____

11. Most benefits claims that are made about equine-assisted therapy are well substantiated through conclusive and high-quality empirical research.

    a. True
    b. False

12. When physical, occupational, or speech therapists incorporate equine movement and the farm milieu in a patient's treatment plan, it is called:

    a. Equine-assisted psychotherapy
    b. Hippotherapy
    c. Adaptive riding
    d. Therapeutic riding

13. Name three ethological needs that must be attended to when caring for horses. _____

    _____

14. A certificate of completion only indicates a person has successfully completed a training program and is not the same as a credential or a certification that is the outcome of a credentialing process.

    a. True
    b. False

15. Biophila is defined as: _____

16. Horses need horse–horse interactions down time and space to roam freely away from humans, even their caregivers and owners.

    a. True
    b. False

17. A non-therapy skills-based service in which specialty trained instructors teach horseback riding and horsemanship skills to students with disabilities or special needs is called:

    _____

18. Therapists can include other people in the therapy session without permission from the patient or the parent or legal guardian.

    a. True
    b. False

19. Is the EAGALA model of equine-assisted psychotherapy indicative or inclusive of all the various ways people might include horses in mental health practice?

    a. Yes
    b. No

20. Why is the term "adaptive riding" preferred to "therapeutic riding" when attempting to differentiate between therapy and non-therapy services? _____

    _____

21. The licensed therapist is responsible for making all clinical decisions during therapy and overseeing the treatment process.

    a. True
    b. False

22. What is the difference between an industry and a field? _____

    _____

23. Providing education and training about equine psychology, physiology, behavior, and communication is an important risk management strategy.

    a. True
    b. False

24. List the common methodological issues found in current equine-assisted therapy research:

    _____

    _____

25. Therapists can abdicate their legal and ethical responsibilities for keeping patients safe or designing clinical activities to a non-licensed horse professional if they don't have horse experience themselves.

    a. True
    b. False

26. List five key components that must be addressed in an informed consent document:

    a. _____

    b. _____

    c. _____

    d. _____

    e. _____

27. It is the legal and ethical responsibility of the licensed healthcare professional to protect the safety, dignity, and confidentiality of the patient during treatment even if equine-assisted therapy is used.

    a. True
    b. False

28. Describe why it is so important to clearly differentiate between therapy and non-therapy services. _____

_____

29. A non-therapy service that focuses on teaching life skills, social skills, communication skills, or leadership skills is called:

    a. Adaptive riding
    b. Equine-assisted psychotherapy
    c. Equine-assisted learning
    d. Equine-facilitated psychotherapy

30. An advanced or additional level of practice beyond the typical scope of knowledge included in a licensed professional's education and training is called:

    a. A treatment strategy
    b. A treatment approach
    c. A treatment intervention
    d. A specialty area of practice

31. List three possible precautions that should be considered when assessing a patient for equine-assisted therapy.

    a. _____

    b. _____

    c. _____

32. Equine-assisted therapy includes adaptive riding.

    a. True
    b. False
    c. _____

33. List three possible contraindications for equine-assisted therapy.

    a. _____

    b. _____

    c. _____

34. Therapeutic riding is the same as hippotherapy, and the two terms can be used interchangeably.

    a. True
    b. False

35. Equine-assisted therapy is more than owning or loving horses. It is a highly nuanced specialty that requires additional training, education, and experience.

    a. True
    b. False

36. Why is collaboration so important for the industry of equine-assisted therapy? _____
    _____

37. Why is it so important that licensed healthcare providers have training and education about equine physiology, psychology, and behavior, as well as specialty training in equine-assisted therapy? _____

    _____

    _____

☐ Answer Key

1. b
2. a, c, d
3. c
4. c
5. Answer can include any of the following:
   a. non-profit or 501 (c)(3) model
   b. private practice or sole proprietor model
   c. hospital or clinic model
   d. for-profit LLC or PLLC
   e. employee or contractor model
6. a
7. e
8. a
9. c
10. Answer can include any of the following:
    a. program description and description of services
    b. administrative plan
    c. market analysis
    d. SWOT analysis
    e. marketing plan
    f. financials (budget/pro forma)
    g. risk management plan
    h. bios/staff make up
11. b
12. b
13. Answer can include any of the following:
    a. horse-horse interactions including free time, grooming, and play
    b. exercise and freedom of movement
    c. shelter/a safe space to sleep, rest, and escape bugs and the elements
    d. food/clean water
    e. healthcare
14. a
15. The innate human tendency to seek connections with nature and other forms of life.
16. a
17. adaptive or "therapeutic" riding
18. b
19. b
20. "adaptive riding" clearly differentiates the service as a non-therapy form of recreational riding lesson, whereas "therapeutic riding" causes confusion due to the similarity with the protected term "therapy".
21. a

22. an "industry" is a commercial endeavor that combines similar businesses and embraces both licensed professionals as well as business owners, technicians, paraprofessionals, and support staff, while a "field" indicates a specific area of professional practice or study.

23. a

24. combing treatment types, lack of clarity around terminology and treatment types, lack of control groups, issues with sample sizes and the generalizability of results, and problems with novel effects and controlling variabilities, measuring outcomes, and practitioner-researcher bias.

25. b

26. Answer can include any of the following:
    a. full disclosure regarding the risks and benefits associated with the treatment or service
    b. the evidence (or lack thereof) supporting the treatment or service
    c. information about how the treatment or service may influence or impact the patient
    d. the unique characteristics of the treatment or service
    e. additional considerations like cost, time, and travel expenses
    f. patient signature—the patient (or his/her parent or legal guardian) must sign this document, indicating he/she is aware of the information, and is agreeing or consenting to treatment

27. a

28. Answers that include patient safety, scope of practice, legality, or ethics are likely acceptable.

29. c

30. d

31. Any three of the following are acceptable:
    a. history of animal abuse
    b. history of fire setting
    c. suspected current or past physical, sexual, and/or emotional abuse
    d. history of seizure disorder,
    e. gross obesity
    f. medication side effects
    g. stress-induced reactive airway disease (asthma)
    h. migraines
    i. joint mobility limitation
    j. height and weight
    k. age (under 3 or elderly)

32. b or possibly c—there are times when adaptive riding can be used as part of a patient's treatment plan *if* the instructor is supervised by a licensed healthcare provider, and that professional creates and oversees the treatment plan and treatment goals.

33. Any three of the following are acceptable:
    a. Actively dangerous to self or others (suicidal, homicidal, aggressive)
    b. actively delirious, demented, dissociative, psychotic, or severely confused (including severe delusion involving horses)
    c. acute herniated disc with or without nerve root compression
    d. actively substance abusing
    e. atlantoaxial instability (AAI)—a displacement of the C1 vertebra in relation to the C2 vertebra as seen on x-ray or computed tomography of significant amount (generally agreed to be greater than 4 mm for a child), with or without neurologic signs as assessed

by a qualified physician; this condition is seen with diagnoses which have ligamentous laxity such as Down syndrome or juvenile rheumatoid arthritis

    f. chiari II malformation with neurologic symptoms

    g. coxa arthrosis—degeneration of the hip joint; the femoral head is flattened and functions like a hinge joint rather than as a ball and socket joint. Sitting on the horse puts extreme stress on the joint

    h. grand mal seizures—uncontrolled by medications

    i. hemophilia with a recent history of bleeding episodes

    j. indwelling urethral catheters

    k. medical conditions during acute exacerbations (rheumatoid arthritis, herniated nucleus pulposis, multiple sclerosis, diabetes, etc.)

    l. open wounds over a weight-bearing surface

    m. pathologic fractures without successful treatment of the underlying pathology (e.g. severe osteoporosis, osteogenesis imperfecta, bone tumor, etc.)

    n. tethered cord with symptoms

    o. unstable spine or joints including unstable internal hardware.

34. b
35. a
36. There is no right or wrong answer to this question. However, answers that include building consensus, having an open mind, working together to advance the industry, and increasing standardization can indicate comprehension of the book's material.
37. There is no right or wrong answer to this question. However, answers that include risk management, professional competency/increasing the chances of the service being effective, or ethics and safety can indicate comprehension of the book's material.

☐ Hands-On Activity: Gratitude and Honoring Our Horses

Description: This activity is an opportunity to give back to your horse. So much of the time we ask horses to help us in accomplishing something we want to do. This is a chance to learn more about our equine partners and honor their feelings, needs, and desires.

Amount of Time: 2–4 hours.

Directions: First watch Louie Schwartzberg's video *Nature. Beauty. Gratitude* (Schwartzberg 2011). It is available for free online. Consider the concept of gratitude and giving back.

Next, spend time with your horse or a horse you work with closely. Through careful observation and trial and error, discover what activity this horse enjoys the most. Put your own needs and expectations aside, and do exactly what the horse likes best. Consider the following options.

- Being groomed by hand or with tools
- Going for a walk with you and exploring somewhere new
- Eating grass and relaxing
- A massage or other form of body work
- Going for a good gallop
- Having social time with other horses
- Getting a bath and then rolling
- Chasing cows or jumping or another high-energy activity that challenges and excites the horse

☐ Journal Entry

Use these questions as an opportunity to explore your own ideas, thoughts, feelings, and personal reflections.

1. What did you learn from your horse about giving back and being grateful, especially for the animals we ask to help us? How might you use this information going forward?

    _____

    _____

    _____

    _____

2. What learning highlights are you taking away from this book and workbook? How will this information inform your clinical practice or change your thoughts or approach to equine-assisted therapy?

    _____

    _____

    _____

    _____

3. Did the results of your "Biases and Beliefs Self-Assessment" change over the three times you took it? What did you learn about yourself in the process?

    _____

    _____

    _____

    _____

4. What is the best gift you can offer the industry of equine-assisted therapy? How can you personally help it to grow and develop in an ethical and safe manner?

    _____

    _____

    _____

    _____

☐ **Resources**

Books & Articles

American Counseling Association (ACA). (2016). *ACA Code of Ethics*. Retrieved from: www.counseling.org/resources/aca-code-of-ethics.pdf

American Occupational Therapy Association (AOTA). (2014). *Scope of Practice*. Retrieved from: http://ajot.aota.org/article.aspx?articleid=1934867

American Physical Therapy Association (APTA). (2016a). *The Physical Therapist Scope of Practice*. Retrieved from: www.apta.org/ScopeOfPractice/

American Physical Therapy Association (APTA). (2016b). *Term and Title Protection*. Retrieved from: www.apta.org/TermProtection/

American Psychological Association (APA). (2006). *Evidence-Based Practice in Psychology*. Retrieved from: www.apa.org/pubs/journals/features/evidence-based-statement.pdf

American Speech-Language-Hearing Association (ASHA). (2017a). *Introduction to Evidence-Based Practice: What It Is (And What It Isn't)*. Retrieved from: www.asha.org/Research/EBP/Introduction-to-Evidence-Based-Practice/

American Speech-Language-Hearing Association (ASHA). (2017b). *Scope of Practice in Speech-Language Pathology*. Retrieved from: www.asha.org/policy/SP2016-00343/

Blue Cross of Idaho. (2017). *Investigational Definition*. Retrieved from: www.bcidaho.com/providers/medical_policies/mp-definitions.asp

Garrison, D.R. (2015). *Thinking collaboratively: Learning in a community of inquiry*. Routledge.

Hanson, M.P. (2005). *Clues to achieving consensus: A leader's guide to navigating collaborative problem solving*. Lanham, MD: Rowman & Littlefield Education.

Kaplan, D.M., & Gladding, S.T. (2011). *A Vision for the Future of Counseling: The 20/20 Principles for Unifying and Strengthening the Profession*. Retrieved from: www.pacounseling.org/aws/PACA/asset_manager/get_file/141519?ver=199

Kaplan, D.M., Tarvydas, V.M., & Gladding, S.T. (2014). *20/20: A Vision for the Future of Counseling: The New Consensus Definition of Counseling*. Retrieved from: www.counseling.org/docs/default-source/david-kaplan's-files/2020-jcd-article.pdf?sfvrsn=2

Matthews, J.H. (2012). Role of professional organizations in advocating for the nursing profession. *Online Journal of Issues in Nursing, 17*(1), 1–10. Retrieved from: http://nursingworld.org/MainMenuCategories/ANAMarketplace/ANAPeriodicals/OJIN/TableofContents/Vol-17-2012/No1-Jan-2012/Professional-Organizations-and-Advocating.html

Pepper, M., & Driscoll, D.L. (2015). *Writing Definitions*. Retrieved from: https://owl.english.purdue.edu/owl/resource/622/01/

Premera. (2017). *Medically Necessary*. Retrieved from: www.premera.com/documents/024773.pdf

Rand Corporation. (2017). *The Delphi Method*. Retrieved from: www.rand.org/topics/delphi-method.html

Straus, S.E., Glasziou, P., Richardson, W.S., & Haynes, R.B. (2010). *Evidence-based medicine: How to practice and teach it* (4th edition). London, UK: Churchill Livingstone.

Video

Schwartzberg, L. (2011). *Nature. Beauty. Gratitude*. Retrieved from: www.ted.com/talks/louie_schwartzberg_nature_beauty_gratitude

Lightning Source UK Ltd.
Milton Keynes UK
UKHW031932251020
372144UK00019B/336

9 781138 216198